Personal Health Records

The Essential Missing Element in 21st Century Healthcare

Holly Dara Miller, MD, MBA, FHIMSS
William A. Yasnoff, MD, PhD, FACMI
Howard A. Burde, Esquire

HIMSS Mission

To lead change in the healthcare information and management systems field through knowledge sharing, advocacy, collaboration, innovation, and community affiliations.

Printed in the U.S.A. 5 4 3 2 1

Requests for permission to reproduce any part of this work should be sent to
Permissions Editor
HIMSS
230 E. Ohio St., Suite 500
Chicago, IL 60611-3270
cmclean@himss.org

ISBN: 978-0-9800697-6-1

For more information about HIMSS, please visit www.himss.org.

About the Authors

Holly Miller, MD, MBA, FHIMSS, is the vice president and CMIO at University Hospitals (UH), a community-based system which serves patients at more than 150 locations throughout Northeast Ohio, including seven wholly-owned and four affiliated hospitals. Dr. Miller is a senior clinical executive at UH and in that role provides leadership and vision for the strategic planning, operations, integration and implementation of information systems and technology that support clinicians and healthcare consumers.

Prior to joining UH, Dr. Miller worked as a health information technology (HIT) managing director for the Cleveland Clinic, where she was responsible for the Personal Health Record, and other eCleveland Clinic services.

Dr. Miller is a frequent presenter at national meetings on HIT and PHRs and is active in healthcare informatics research pertaining to the use of HIT and PHRs for medical condition management and health maintenance.

Dr. Miller is currently a member of the HIMSS Board of Directors. She has been active in the Society's PHR activities and formerly served as chair of the HIMSS PHR Steering Committee, and as one of the ten physician leaders of the Physician Steering Committee for the HIMSS Physician Community, a joint venture of HIMSS and the Association of Medical Directors of Information Systems (AMDIS). Dr. Miller is a former member of the Public Programs Implementation Taskforce and the Health Care Practice Taskforce of the National Governors Association State Alliance for e-Health. In 2008, she was appointed to the Ohio Health Information Partnership Advisory Board by Governor Ted Strickland. In 2008, she served on the Certification

Commission for Healthcare Information Technology (CCHIT) PHR Advisory Task Force. In 2007 she was selected as one of the 50 Most Powerful Physician Executives by *Modern Physician* magazine.

Dr. Miller previously lived in France where she served as a project leader for Ciba-Geigy's clinical phase III and IV trials in gynecology and cardiology. Dr. Miller earned her MBA at Groupe HEC, Paris, France.

William A. Yasnoff, MD, PhD, FACMI, a well-known national leader in health informatics, is founder and managing partner of NHII Advisors, a consulting firm that helps communities and organizations successfully develop health information infrastructure systems and solutions.

Previously, Dr. Yasnoff was senior advisor to NHII at the U.S. Department of Health and Human Services. In that role, he initiated and organized the activities leading to the President's $50 million FY05 budget request and creation of the Office of the National Coordinator for Health Information Technology, establishing the NHII as a widely recognized national goal. Prior to that, Dr. Yasnoff spent five years at the Centers for Disease Control, where he became well known for his work in public health informatics, including co-editing the textbook, *Public Health Informatics and Information Systems*.

Earlier, Dr. Yasnoff developed and deployed Oregon's statewide immunization registry, which is still operating successfully today. He is an associate editor of the *Journal of Biomedical Informatics*, adjunct professor of health sciences informatics at Johns Hopkins University and health management and systems sciences at the University of Louisville. Dr. Yasnoff was a board member of the American Medical Informatics Association in 2003–2004 and is the author of over 250 publications and presentations, including the "Health Information Infrastructure and Public Health Informatics" chapter in the third edition of the widely-used textbook, *Biomedical Informatics: Computer Applications in Healthcare and Medicine*. Dr. Yasnoff earned his PhD in computer science and MD from Northwestern, was elected a fellow of the American College of Medical Informatics in 1989 and was recognized for his achievements with an honorary DrPH in 2006 from the University of Louisville.

Howard Burde, Esquire, is a partner and Chair of the Health Law Practice at Blank Rome LLP, where he represents health information technology companies, health plans, and federal, state, and local governments. He routinely counsels in the areas of HIT; health insurance and managed care law issues; licensure; and certification and accreditation matters.

Mr. Burde's wealth of health law knowledge, developed over 20 years of practice, includes seven years of service as Deputy General Counsel to Governors Tom Ridge and Mark Schweiker of Pennsylvania. In this position, he served as legal counsel for Commonwealth of Pennsylvania responsible for the Departments of Health, Public Welfare and Aging, the Health Related Professional Boards and the Medical Professional Liability Catastrophe Loss Fund. He also advised on all managed care, health insurance, public health, professional liability, and health and human service issues. Prior to his government service, Mr. Burde had seven years of private practice experience representing healthcare providers. Mr. Burde is editor and contributing author of three books: *A Guide to Establishing RHIOs* (HIMSS, 2007); *The Utilization Management Guide* (URAC, 2004); and *The Health Laws of Pennsylvania* (PBI Press, 2001), as well as the author of several articles on health law.

Mr. Burde is on the editorial boards of the *Journal of Health Law* and the *BNA Health Law Reporter*. He serves as attorney on the National Governor's Association State Alliance for E-Health, and was recently appointed to the bipartisan Joint Committee for the Revision of Health Laws in Pennsylvania. Mr. Burde is a frequent speaker on health law topics to audiences including HIMSS, Capitol Hill Steering Committee on Health Informatics, the American Health Lawyers Association, the Utilization Review Accreditation Commission, the Health Care Financial Management Association, the Milbank Memorial Fund, the Hospital Association of Pennsylvania, the Managed Care Association of Pennsylvania, and the Pennsylvania Bar Institute, as well as to client customer and user groups. He is on the Boards of HIMSS, Teach for America, and the Center for Autism (the latter of which he is pro bono counsel). Mr. Burde is a graduate of the University of Virginia School of Law, where he founded the Virginia Health Law Forum, and of Duke University, where he was a baccalaureate speaker at graduation.

Contents

Foreword

By Blackford Middleton, MD, MPH, MSc, FACP, FACMI, FHIMSS
Chairman, Center for Information Technology Leadership
Corporate Director, Clinical Informatics Research & Development
Partners HealthCare System
Harvard Medical School
Boston, MA

It is a pleasure for me to write the foreword for this new book on Personal Health Records by Dr. Holly Miller, Dr. Bill Yasnoff, and Mr. Howard Burde. The authors have produced an insightful and valuable book that provides a comprehensive overview of many of the issues pertaining to the adoption and use of personal health records (PHRs) in this country. Healthcare information technology (HIT) is described as an essential component of healthcare reform and transformation; PHRs are a critical part of HIT that will transform healthcare. If you want to know how and why, read this book.

Personal Health Records: Why Now?

Medicine and information technology both continue to advance at a blistering pace. The innovations of modern medical practice boggle the mind of any clinician: we can now visualize almost any tissue and organ *in vivo;* we have mapped the human genome and are rapidly advancing our understanding of the genetic and proteomic basis of disease; we have a pharmacopeia that has an agent to treat almost any ailment and many 'lifestyle' type agents which aim to improve our human condition; and in the Western world at least, we are living longer and generally better than ever before. If these advances boggle our minds, imagine how our patients must feel.

Information technology also continues to advance dramatically. We now can essentially communicate verbally and visually with anyone around the world who owns a computer and has an Internet connection. Our portable computers now have the processing power and storage capacity that only a few years ago we obtained only in mainframe or mini-computers. The world-wide Web has emerged as the world's online library of an extraordinary array of knowledge, computing tools and resources, and media, and which may enable a social network that spans the globe. Soon, our phones will have comparable processing power and we will essentially have virtual access to the entire world-wide Web, and to each other, anywhere, at anytime.

Medicine at a Crossroads: Costs, Quality, Patient Safety

Despite these advances, however, in medicine and information technology, we see that healthcare in the Western world is characterized by problems with access, a maldistribution of resources, inequities in care, unexplained variation in care patterns, problems with medical error, poor quality, and a continuing escalation in costs of care that have defied various efforts at cost control. In the developing world, the situation is even more challenging due to lack of basic healthcare infrastructure and insufficient resources to apply toward healthcare. These problems have prompted the public and private payor community to begin to clamp down on healthcare costs through a wide variety of mechanisms, some more like a blunt instrument, and other more nuanced efforts at cost control and management. Nevertheless, these efforts have only slightly attenuated the spiraling costs of healthcare.

In a landmark series of reports on healthcare costs and quality and information technology, the Institute of Medicine suggested that a computer-based patient record was an essential part of healthcare reform. Great progress has been made in understanding the promise and perils of HIT— how it may help control costs, improve outcomes, and improve the processes of care delivery, but it is also clear that HIT may cause unexpected and untoward outcomes when used, either through flaws in design, inappropriate implementation or use, or simply the lack of experience among new users. Nevertheless, HIT is rightly viewed as part of the solution for what ails healthcare for the evidence would suggest that appropriate use of HIT can reduce medical errors, improve the quality of care and healthcare outcomes, and reduce the costs of care.

Yet HIT is only slowly being adopted in the U.S. This observer would suggest that the slow adoption of HIT is largely due to a market failure for HIT in this country. That is, the benefits that accrue using HIT do not flow to the person or entity that has made the investment in HIT. For example, if an EMR prevents an adverse drug event through alerting about a potential drug-drug interaction, or even worse, an allergy condition, the doctor using the EMR can change course and avoid the untoward outcome. However, the costs saved from that patient not having an adverse drug event or, even worse, presenting to the emergency department, flow to the payor for that patient's healthcare, whether public or private. Yet the payor did not make the investment in the EMR which helped avoid the problem in the first place. This asymmetry of risk and reward is clear to physicians, and is one of the main reasons for the slow adoption of HIT, especially in the small office care setting.

Patient-Centered Care, Mobile Consumerism, and the "Silver Tsunami"

The PHR is a critical part of the solution that overcomes this log-jam. We are in the midst of one of the most dramatic demographic shifts of all time as the baby-boomer cohort ages, develops multiple chronic conditions, and raises expectations for service and convenience in healthcare services similar to what it has received in all other sectors of the economy. The pressure for improving the management of chronic diseases in a growing aged population segment places increased pressure on the healthcare delivery system for cost containment, efficiency, and effectiveness of care. The public and private payors are now considering ways in which PHR may help them contain costs and manage chronic diseases more effectively—with or without the engagement of the patient's providers in some cases.

These activities may actually be the stimulus required to prompt the provider community to reconsider EMR adoption more aggressively, especially if combined with payor incentives to adopt HIT. The evidence is mixed, but it may be that ultimately the best means by which a complicated elderly patient can be managed is by a provider using an EMR, and a patient participating in their care by using a PHR, which shares data and communicates with the provider's EMR. Renewed efforts to uphold and maintain the long-term therapeutic relationship between provider and patient, including the ideas surrounding the medical home and related patient-centered care efforts, demonstrate how the provider community is responding to the need for cost containment, improved quality, and an increasingly technology savvy consumer who is demanding convenience, service, and high quality.

Technology Innovation: EMR, EHR, and PHR

Lastly, the time for PHRs has come because we have seen extraordinary innovation in information technology in many service sectors, and it is finally coming to healthcare! The sophistication and security of information technology now used in a ubiquitous manner in banking, travel, shopping, online media, social networking, and etc., demonstrates the value and utility of information technology. Now, several large healthcare delivery systems that have been able to make the investment in HIT, such as the Veteran's Administration, Kaiser Permanente, and others, have demonstrated that these technologies can dramatically decrease the costs and increase the quality of care at scale, across an entire healthcare delivery system, for millions of patients. As the technology infrastructure is established on the provider side, this can be leveraged to facilitate patient access to healthcare information, their own medical records, and communicate with their own provider team, and possibly others with conditions similar to their own. Just as we now see our brokerage accounts seamlessly interoperating with our banking accounts, we may see finally the seamless interoperation of multiple provider PHRs interoperating with a patient-controlled PHR.

What Is Good about This Book?

This book is a delight to read: it is well written, to the point, uses examples where appropriate to help illustrate a point, and is well referenced with pointers to the primary academic and market literature where appropriate. It also examines the perspectives of various stakeholders in the PHR puzzle, notably the patient, of course, but also the provider, and the payor. Most importantly, however, the book is comprehensive: it provides a lucid discussion of many of the issues pertaining to the adoption and use of PHRs in this country. While not every issue can be discussed in exhaustive detail, key topics are presented so that the reader may come away with a broad understanding of the issues pertaining to PHR.

Topics discussed include:
- Privacy, confidentiality, and security
- Predictive modeling
- Web 2.0, social networking
- New patient-provider paradigm
- Public trust
- Practical implementation guidelines: project planning and budgeting
- PHR laws
- PHR business and sustainability models

Any reader who wants additional information beyond what is discussed in this book may turn to the references for additional reading and understanding.

Who Is the Audience for This Book?

This book is for anyone with an interest in personal health records. The broad scope of the book and the accessible writing style make it appropriate for the lay reader, a patient, or someone considering using a PHR to help care for a loved one, as well as clinicians interested in obtaining an understanding of the issues pertaining to adoption and use of PHRs. Clinical informaticians, IT professionals, and HIT professionals will also find this a useful book for the overview it provides of many issues pertaining to PHR.

Enjoy learning about PHRs by reading this book.

Preface

In 2003, when one of the authors first gave a presentation on personal health records to a group of CIOs, there was a resounding lack of credulity in the room that personal health records (PHRs) would ever catch on. The essence of the response was, why would a healthcare organization want to offer a PHR? Now Kaiser Permanente has over 2,200,000 registered users.

Many healthcare information technology (HIT) groups have demonstrated a growing interest in PHRs. Citing some examples of this interest among many are HIMSS' inauguration of a PHR Steering Committee in 2006; HL7 developing PHR-related use cases in 2007; the Markle Foundation convening a group of industry experts regarding PHRs in 2007; CCHIT assuming the task of certifying PHRs, with a major focus on PHR privacy and security; and AHIC devoting the majority of a meeting to mobilizing consumers' personal health information, from both the consumer and industry perspectives. Several HIT groups have published PHR definitions, including the Markle Foundation, HIMSS and AMIA, and most recently NAHIT.

Many electronic medical record (EMR) vendors have developed PHR-accompanying products, and patients most frequently review their test results and communicate with their physicians using these tethered systems. Payors are increasingly offering PHRs; employers are interested in their employees using PHRs. There are a variety of stand-alone commercial PHRs available including condition-specific PHRs. Industry giants have made their first forays into healthcare with the development and release of PHRs and/or PHR platforms. The promise of such platforms is to allow consumers to aggregate their health information and to control the flow of the health information exchange.

To date there is not an abundance of peer-reviewed literature regarding which consumers are accessing PHRs and what the benefits are to these consumers.

In 2007, HIMSS requested the authors to write a book on PHRs. This text is the result, and is meant to serve as a primer and a vision for PHRs. It is intended for readers who desire a basic introduction to the concepts, principles, and short history of this rapidly evolving area of health IT.

This book is a collaboration of three authors, Dr. Holly Miller, Dr. William Yasnoff and Howard Burde, each of whom is drawn to the promise of PHRs for healthcare transformation but approach this subject from a different perspective.

As with any book, Dr. Miller, Dr. Yasnoff and Mr. Burde are merely the names on the front and the content providers. The book itself is a result of the contributions of numerous others who gave their time and effort and we thank them here.

Dr. Miller would like to thank the HIMSS PHR Steering Committee, the HIMSS staff, her HIT mentors, and her family who put up with her working on the book on weekends.

Dr. Yasnoff would like to thank Helga Rippen, MD, PhD, MPH, who was instrumental in persuading him of the potential of patient-controlled PHRs, and Dr. Bill Dodd, retired general practitioner from Scotland, who first proposed the idea of a repository or "health record bank" to the U.K. National Health Service in 1997. He is truly a visionary who was far ahead of his time.

Mr. Burde would like to thank his assistant, Lauren Nuttle, and the night typing staff at Blank Rome's Word Processing Center. He would also like to thank his colleagues who unwittingly agreed to permit him to devote substantial time to publishing yet another book. Their forbearance is appreciated.

Dr. Miller, Dr. Yasnoff and Mr. Burde would also like to thank Fran Perveiler, Mary Griskiewicz, Dave Roberts, Pat Wise, Carla Smith, and all of our other friends and colleagues at the Healthcare Information and Management Systems Society for their patience and support.

Holly D. Miller, MD, MBA, FHIMSS
William A. Yasnoff, MD, PhD, FACMI
Howard A. Burde, Esquire

CHAPTER 1

Need for ePHRs to Address Critical Problems in U.S. Healthcare

Despite extraordinary advances in medicine and the exponential growth in knowledge of diseases, their processes and treatments, the U.S. healthcare system is broken:

- We are experiencing an epidemic of largely preventable diseases.
- The largest segment of the population, the baby boomers, is aging and steadily requiring additional healthcare resources.
- Healthcare costs are significantly increasing.
- The number of employers not providing insurance to their employees is increasing significantly, as is the number of uninsured.
- National healthcare quality in the U.S. lags behind most other industrialized nations, despite the fact that healthcare costs in the U.S. exceed those of all other industrialized nations.

The U.S. healthcare system is at a crossroads. Despite many opinions on how the above dilemmas are to be solved, most of the constituents invested in solving the U.S. healthcare crisis believe that two factors will play a critical role: the use of health information technology (HIT) and engagement of healthcare consumers regarding their healthcare choices, health-related behaviors and chronic care management. The electronic personal health record (ePHR) is the intersection of HIT and consumer engagement in health and wellness. As such, it is a tool that can help solve our current healthcare crisis of costs, preventable diseases and the need for quality improvements by promoting healthy behaviors, focusing consumers on preventative medicine and encouraging compliance with medical regimens for existing illnesses.

THE U.S. HEALTHCARE SYSTEM IS BROKEN

Epidemic of Preventable Disease

An "epidemic" is defined as an unprecedented incidence of new cases of a disease. We are suffering from an epidemic of preventable diseases such as obesity, heart disease and diabetes. This epidemic is rampant in all generations—from the baby boomers and older to our children and adolescents. For example, the prevalence of obesity in the U.S. has become a public health problem so serious that our nation has the highest rates of obesity in the developed world. From 1980 to 2002, the incidence of obesity has doubled in adults and the number of overweight children and adolescents has tripled.[1] The frequency of lifestyle-related diseases also continues to rise; for example, the rate of diagnosed diabetes increased 43 percent, up from 4.9 per 1000/population in 1997 to 7.0 per 1000/population in 2004. Even after adjusting for age, the incidence increased 41 percent, suggesting that the majority of the change was not due to the aging of the population.[2] In fact, given the increased prevalence of poor nutritional habits and obesity in our children and adolescents, it is likely that this generation may have a greater occurrence of chronic disease as they age than experienced by the baby boomer generation.

Aging Population

Current statistics demonstrate that patients age 65 and older visit their doctors an average nine times per year and that two-thirds of this population has one or more chronic diseases.[3,4,5] As the baby boomers age, by the year 2030, the national population of individuals

65 and older will grow from 35 million in 2000 to 71.5 million people, representing nearly a fifth of the total U.S. population.[6]

Healthcare Costs

Given our current healthcare resources, the challenge of providing healthcare to the aging baby boomers is daunting; indeed, the associated costs alone are overwhelming. It is predicted that national healthcare spending as a percentage of the U.S. gross domestic product (GDP) will continue to rise from five percent of GDP in 1960 to 21 percent of GDP by the year 2020.[7] In addition, the U.S. spends nearly twice as much per capita on healthcare as most other industrialized nations.[8]

Healthcare Quality

Yet, despite this level of spending for healthcare in the U.S., our life expectancy is exceeded by 21 other countries; infant mortality is the fifth highest of any industrialized nation; and we have more cancer cases per 100,000 people reported in the U.S. than in half of other industrialized nations.[9] A report based on two surveys of adult patients' views and experiences of their healthcare system in five developed Anglophone nations found that the U.S. system ranked first on measures of provision and receipt of preventive or "right" care, but came in last on all other dimensions of quality, including chronic care management and safe, coordinated and patient-centered care. In particular, the U.S. performed poorly in terms of providing care equitably, safely, efficiently or in a patient-centered manner. In addition, the U.S. ranked last with poor scores in all three indicators of healthy lives (healthcare access, quality, and efficiency). For all countries, responses indicated room for improvement; yet, the other four countries spend considerably less than the U.S. on healthcare per person and as a percent of GDP.[10]

Healthcare Insurance

Many other developed nations that rank higher in surveys of healthcare quality than the U.S. have some form of single payor system. In the

U.S., most people have health insurance through employer-sponsored plans. In fact, this is considered, "…a cornerstone of the U.S. health care system, as vital in some ways to the health care of Americans as the drugs, devices, and medical services that the insurance covers. Employer-sponsored insurance has been described as the equivalent of 'private social security,' and if it were suddenly to disappear, chaos would certainly result: the health of patients throughout the United States would be jeopardized, and physicians' income would plummet."[11]

In 2006, 59.7 percent of Americans were covered by an employer-sponsored health insurance plan and 67.9 percent were covered by a private plan. These numbers are falling. Both of these percentages have significantly decreased statistically from the respective 2005 figures of 60.2 percent and 68.5 percent. Americans covered by Medicare and Medicaid also slightly decreased from 2005 to 2006, but not very significantly (13.6 percent in 2005, and 12.9 percent in 2006, respectively). The percent of Americans without health insurance is increasing: from 2005 to 2006, the percent of uninsured Americans significantly increased statistically with the 2006 percent of uninsured at 15.8 percent, compared to 15.3 percent in 2005.[12]

The main reason for the increasing numbers of uninsured is the skyrocketing cost of healthcare. The U.S. is spending far more for the same healthcare goods and services than other developed nations. "The United States is spending more on health care per capita than any other country, but its use of medical services—measured by, for example, hospital days and physician visits per capita—is below the Organization for Economic Co-operation and Development (OECD) median. This suggests that prices could be much higher in the United States than in other countries."[13] And with more and more Americans uninsured, families will be even less likely to receive preventive care, thereby further contributing to healthcare cost escalation down the road.

INCREMENTAL OR "BIG BANG"?

While it is clear that something must change, it is hard to predict whether that change will come as a "big bang" or will occur incrementally. This has become a frequent recent topic of conversation within HIT circles.

While the discussion continues, incremental change is happening all the time. Managed care was introduced to change the focus of healthcare from episodic-based acute and tertiary disease care to one of primary care and preventive medicine. In response to this model, there was a backlash among some managed care recipients who felt that their conditions were undertreated. Despite this attempted shift, healthcare costs in the U.S. continued to rise, as did America's rates of preventable disease.

Now, a focus on the quality of care is being promoted. The Joint Commission requires core measures of quality to be publicly reported by accredited hospitals. The Centers for Medicare and Medicaid Services (CMS), "…is developing and implementing a set of pay-for-performance initiatives to support quality improvement in the care of Medicare beneficiaries. In addition to the initiatives for hospitals, physicians and physician groups described below, CMS is also exploring opportunities in nursing home care—building on the progress of the Nursing Home Quality Initiative—and is considering approaches for home health and dialysis providers as well. Finally, recognizing that many of the best opportunities for quality improvement are patient-focused and cut across settings of care, CMS is pursuing pay-for-performance (P4P) initiatives to support better care coordination for patients with chronic illnesses."[14]

It is well documented that these changes do affect the behaviors of providers in their care of patients as demonstrated by a January 2007 article in the *New York Times*. The article stated that "the 266 hospitals participating in a Medicare experiment that pays them more to follow medical recommendations have steadily improved the quality of patient care."[15] But in order to affordably achieve the reporting needed to fulfill The Joint Commission and CMS requirements above, healthcare providers must have HIT systems in place.

HIT is the key component of the infrastructure providers require in order to realize improvements in quality measures and participate in P4P financial incentives. HIT systems transform the required reporting process from a labor intensive and costly manual process to one that is automated. In addition, some systems have tools that support providers in their practice of evidenced-based medicine, the foundation of the CMS quality measures. This will very likely prove to be the final push to encourage the use of HIT systems by all healthcare providers.

TECHNOLOGY AND THE INTERNET ARE TRANSFORMING HEALTHCARE

Technology—specifically the Internet—has, and will continue to have, a huge impact on our society and every aspect of our lives. Though healthcare has been slower to embrace technology than other industries like banking and retail, there are forces at play that are moving the healthcare industry to this transition. Indeed, the HIT industry itself has been incrementally maturing.

HIT systems have developed to the point that it is not only possible to have health information seamlessly flow throughout a large and complex independent delivery network (IDN) with multiple sites, but also throughout an entire healthcare provider community, urban area, state and beyond. While the development of standards for data, HIT implementation, interfaces, etc., make this process less costly and more efficient, the current limitations of the application of HIT systems are typically political rather than technical. Healthcare, like any other industry, is competitive. Providers want to leverage the significant investments they have made in HIT systems in order to differentiate themselves and gain competitive advantage in their marketplaces. Such competitive advantage is temporary as HIT is in the process of being widely disseminated across provider organizations and the rest of the healthcare constituencies.[16] HIT, however, is necessary for any organization to be a player in the healthcare industry as the data in HIT systems can be used to:

- Meet requirements for public reporting of performance and outcomes;
- Drive economies of scale and business planning;
- Conduct research, leading to increased prestige for the organization and increased grant funds;
- Generate reports for practice management;
- Improve quality and safety of care, enabling competitive marketing; and
- Offer views and outreach tools to patients to foster their loyalty.

Sharing this data with other provider organizations, or even allowing the healthcare consumer to control the flow of the data, would mean that the provider organization loses some (actual or perceived) competitive advantage. Despite the fact that HIT clearly enables healthcare transformation, it alone is not sufficient to achieve the required transformation of healthcare in the U.S. The financial motivation of healthcare constituents must be managed such that everyone is stimulated to decrease overall healthcare costs in the U.S., while providing medicine of the highest quality, best outcomes and lowest associated morbidities and mortalities.

Despite the advantages of using HIT, the national adoption of electronic record systems is minimal. A 2008 study, sponsored by the Office of the National Coordinator for Health Information Technology (ONC) of the Department of Health and Human Services (HHS), found that only 4 percent of a random sample of U.S. physicians in ambulatory practices reported using a fully functional electronic record system (full) and 13 percent reported using a basic system (basic). Seventy-one percent of the physicians using a full system reported that it was integrated with a hospital system where they admit patients. Doctors using full systems were significantly more likely to have their systems offer personal health record (PHR) functionality to their patients as compared to those using basic systems. Physicians using electronic record systems reported their impressions that the systems improved their quality of care and provided them with higher levels of satisfaction. Financial barriers were noted to be the highest barrier to electronic record adoption.[17]

There have been many recommendations and efforts to stimulate HIT adoption over the last several years. In 2008, CMS launched a program paying 100 physicians with ambulatory practices in each of 12 communities across the nation to report quality measures using electronic medical records. Technology and the Internet are transforming healthcare, but to date that transformation has been slower than hoped for. Clinician adoption across the spectrum of care environments is essential for this transformation to occur. Ultimately, electronic medical record (EMR) adoption by independent practitioners may be driven by consumer adoption of PHRs.

THE HEALTHCARE CONSUMER

The Internet has also dramatically changed the lives of U.S. healthcare consumers. This technological advancement has been adopted more quickly and broadly than several major innovations such as radio, telephone and television. A Pew 2007 survey found that most American homes, regardless of whether they live in an urban or rural setting, now have Internet access. Most of these home Internet users have a broadband connection. According to this survey of 2,200 adult Americans conducted in February and March of 2007:[18]

- Forty-seven percent of all adult Americans have a broadband connection at home, a five percentage point increase from early 2006.
- Among individuals who use the Internet at home, 70 percent have a broadband connection while only 23 percent use dial-up.
- Home broadband adoption in rural areas, while at 31 percent, continues to lag with high speed adoption in urban centers and suburbs.
    - Internet usage in rural areas also trails the national average; 60 percent of rural adults use the Internet from any location, compared with the national average of 71 percent.
- 40 percent of African Americans now have a broadband connection at home, a nine percentage point increase from early 2006.
    - Since 2005, the percentage of African American adults with a home broadband connection has nearly tripled, from 14 percent in early 2005 to 40 percent in early 2007.

In ever-increasing numbers, Americans are using the Internet to look for health information. For example, a series of tracking surveys by the Pew Internet & American Life Project found that 80 percent of online Americans reported that they look for health and medical information on the Internet.[19] This technological savvy has affected Americans' attitudes about EMRs. A September 2006 Wall Street Journal Online/Harris Interactive Health-Care Poll found that the vast majority of patients want to use Internet-based solutions to communicate with their doctors and manage their health information. Patients "…say that they would like to have access to electronic medical records (EMR) and other electronic means of communicating and transferring medical information. If given a choice between a doctor who provides such services and one who does not, more than half of all adults believe this would influence their choice of doctors."[20]

Over a year later, a November, 2007 Wall Street Journal Online/ Harris Interactive Health-Care Poll found that "A sizable majority of Americans believe electronic medical records have the potential to improve U.S. health care and that the benefits outweigh privacy risks." This opinion is clearly divided as illustrated by the fact that a substantial minority (40 percent) did not agree. Privacy protection must clearly be part of any plan to increase adoption of ePHRs.

But this figure does not mitigate the majority view of those who responded that electronic health systems and sharing information from electronic systems could result in better care, decrease medical errors and reduce healthcare costs. Further, the survey showed that a vast majority of Americans want access to their health information, stating that "...91 percent of those polled say patients should have access to their own electronic records maintained by their physician."[21]

The power of technology is hard to deny. In a relatively very brief period of time, the Internet has enabled healthcare consumers to access layperson-friendly medical information. And consumers are using this information to make informed healthcare decisions. Knowledge is power and consumers have empowered themselves through the Internet.

This consumer empowerment is affecting the traditional physician-patient relationship. Traditionally a paternalistic model of medicine, the model is slowly evolving to one in which each healthcare consumer is his or her own healthcare advocate. Along with this role modification from passive recipient to actively engaged consumer, there are trends toward increasing consumer responsibilities regarding their healthcare and health-related behaviors. Above, we discussed that technology functions as a catalyst for change. Adding a catalyst to a chemical reaction does not change the outcome of the reaction, but it greatly speeds up the time frame. The ePHR is the technical tool that will enable healthcare consumers to manage their health and their health-related behaviors in the 21st century.

The purpose of this book is to discuss the current and future state of PHRs and how these technical tools can be used to positively impact U.S. healthcare. The topics that will be covered include:

- Defining the ePHR and other interrelated HIT tools;
- An assessment of the drivers for PHR adoption and barriers to adoption of consumer and provider healthcare constituents;
- The features and functions that PHRs will provide to enable healthcare consumers to manage their healthcare in the face of the changing market forces confronting consumers;
- Some practical considerations for PHR implementation;
- PHR architecture models;
- The evolving legal environment related to PHRs;
- PHR privacy and security; and
- Considerations of the financial sustainability of PHRs.

REFERENCES

1. Ogden C, Carroll M, Curtin L, McDowell M, Tabak C, Flegal K. Prevalence of overweight and obesity in the United States, 1999 - 2004. *JAMA*. 2006; 295:1549-1555. PMID 16595758.
2. Centers for Disease Control. Crude and age-adjusted incidence of diagnosed diabetes per 1000 population aged 18-79 years, United States, 1980–2005. Available at: http://www.cdc.gov/diabetes/statistics/incidence/fig2.htm. Accessed June 11, 2008.
3. Medina C, Migliaccio J. *77 Truths about Marketing to the 50+ Consumer.* CD Publications, 2004.
4. Alliance for Aging Research. Report: Will You Still Treat Me When I'm 65? The National Shortage of Geriatricians. May, 1996.
5. Older American Report: Administration on Aging Makes Case for Greater Senior Independent Living. Business Publishers, Inc. March 17, 2006.
6. Federal Interagency Forum on Aging Related Statistics. Older Americans 2008: Key Indicators of Well-Being. Federal Interagency Forum on Aging Related Statistics. Washington. DC: U.S. Government Printing Office. March, 2008.
7. Anderson GF, et al. Health spending in the United States and the rest of the industrialized world. *Health Affairs* 2005; 24(4):903–914 (published online 17 July 17, 2007).
8. Kaiser Family Foundation. Healthcare spending in the United States and OECD countries. Available at: http://www.kff.org/insurance/snapshot/chcm010307oth.cfm. Accessed June 11, 2008.
9. Institute of Medicine. *Crossing the Quality Chasm: A Health System for the Twenty-first Century.* Washington, DC: National Academies Press; 2001.

10. Davis K, Schoen C, Schoenbaum SC, Audet AJ, Doty MM, Holmgren AL, Kriss JL. *Mirror, Mirror on the Wall: An Update on the Quality of American Health Care Through the Patient's Lens.* The Commonwealth Fund; April, 2006.

11. Blumenthal D. Employer-sponsored health insurance in the United States — Origins and implications. [*N Engl J Med* Web site]. July 6, 2006. Available at: http://content.nejm.org/cgi/content/full/355/1/82. Accessed June 11, 2008. Password required.

12. U.S. Census Bureau. Income, poverty, and health insurance coverage in the United States: 2006. Available at: http://www.census.gov/prod/2007pubs/p60-233.pdf. Accessed June 11, 2008.

13. Anderson GF, et al. Health care spending and use of information technology in OECD countries. *Health Affairs.* 2006; 25(3):819-831.

14. Centers for Medicare and Medicaid Services. Details for Medicare "pay for performance" initiatives [press release]. Available at: http://www.cms.hhs.gov/apps/media/press/release.asp?Counter=1343. Accessed June 11, 2008.

15. Abelson R. Bonus pay by Medicare lifts quality. *The New York Times.* January 25, 2007.

16. Carr NG. IT doesn't matter. *Harvard Business Review.* May 1, 2003.

17. DesRoches, et al., Electronic health records in ambulatory care—A national survey of physicians. *N Engl J Med.* 2008; 359:50-60.

18. Horrigan JB, Smith A. *Home Broadband Adoption, 2007.* Pew Internet and American Life Project. June, 2007.

19. Fox S. Online Health Search, 2006. Pew Internet and American Life Project. October 29, 2006.

20. Cummings J, ed. Few patients use or have access to online services for communicating with their doctors, but most would like to. *Wall Street Journal Online/Harris Interactive.* 2006:5(16). Available at: http://www.harrisinteractive.com/news/newsletters/wsjhealthnews/WSJOnline_HI_Health-CarePoll2006vol5_iss16.pdf. Accessed June 11, 2008.

21. Bright B. Wall Street Journal Online/Harris Interactive Healthcare Poll: Benefits of electronic health records seen as outweighing risks. *Wall Street Journal Online.* November 29, 2007. Available at: http://online.wsj.com/public/article_print/SB119565244262500549.html. Accessed June 11, 2008.

CHAPTER 2

Personal Health Record: History and Context

Despite the fact that HIT is a relatively young industry, it continues to see rapid advancement. The demand for software systems has dramatically increased providers' investment in HIT; software vendors have been consolidating; and the brisk development of new products as well as enhancements of existing products are taking place. There are more and more groups within both the public and private sectors committed to HIT; some of these groups are membership organizations (e.g., the Healthcare Information and Management Systems Society—HIMSS), while some are federally supported (e.g., the American Health Information Community—AHIC). The activities of these groups may span across the HIT industry or they may be dedicated to a specific task such as establishing HIT industry standards.

HIT has never been more important, as improving healthcare quality and decreasing costs will require an organized, private and secure flow of electronic healthcare data throughout all of the healthcare constituents' systems. Most particularly, it will involve flowing all of the data to a consumer-controlled ePHR. Currently, the flow of the electronic healthcare data is in disarray. A consumer's healthcare data, if electronically available at all, exists in multiple disparate systems that are unable to "talk" to each other or to aggregate the data. Most systems and vendors have unique data models; there is no unified single comprehensive healthcare data model to facilitate health information exchange. Health Information Portability and Accountability Act (HIPAA) legislation was passed mandating that healthcare consumers have the right to access their healthcare data and to limit access by others. However, although the data may be available in a digitized format, the consumers may not be able to access the data electronically, let alone determine with whom or with what systems they choose to share their data.

Because this industry is young, many frequently used terms are not yet clearly defined. The same term may mean something very different to different groups or individuals. Before we review the definitions of several key HIT terms, we begin with a brief description of the various offerings that have been described as ePHRs.

PERSONAL HEALTH RECORDS: AN HISTORICAL PERSPECTIVE

Shortly after the birth of Internet search functionality, consumers began trolling the Web for health information. Many healthcare consumer Web sites were formed such as WebMD.com and DrKoop.com. Providers too created Web sites directed to consumers—large healthcare organizations created "brochure-ware" Web sites, maintained by marketing departments, that advertised the services of the provider organization. From simple brochure-ware, these sites evolved to allow consumers to interact with the organization electronically for certain services such as requesting appointments.

Today, each person's medical records are scattered among all their providers, leaving no one provider with a complete copy. Some of these records, or parts of the records, are in electronic format; however, the majority of the records continue to be paper-based. Remarkably, there are no healthcare institutions responsible for ensuring that complete records are available for each person when care is needed. Each person is left to compile the record individually, by requesting their records from the institutions where they have been treated. The safety, quality and efficiency of healthcare could all be greatly improved if complete electronic health records (EHRs) were immediately available when healthcare is provided.

GROWING NATIONAL ATTENTION TO HIT

Back in 1991, the Institute of Medicine (IOM) called the EHR "an essential technology for patient care" in its report, *The Computer-Based Patient Record: An Essential Technology for Patient Care.*[1] Although that report spurred considerable action and some progress in the 1990s, it was the *To Err is Human* report[2] from the IOM in 1999 that really focused the attention of the nation on the pervasive problems of safety and quality in our healthcare system, largely traceable to the limited application of modern information management. That report estimated that medical errors result in between 44,000 and 98,000 preventable deaths each year in hospitals alone. A more recent study showed that only 55 percent of U.S. adults were receiving recommended care.[3]

This was further elucidated and emphasized in subsequent reports from the IOM[4,5] and other national expert panels including the President's Information Technology Advisory Committee[6,7] and the Computer Science and Telecommunications Board of the National Research Council.[8] In 2001, the National Committee on Vital and Health Statistics (NCVHS), a statutory advisory committee to the U.S. Department of Health and Human Services (HHS), explicitly recommended development of a National Health Information Infrastructure (NHII).[9] By then, it had been recognized that EHR systems alone were not enough—the systems would need to interconnect and communicate to ensure that patient information, dispersed among the various places where care had been given, were assembled into a complete record immediately available at any point-of-care. It was also clear that modern information management was an essential prerequisite to improving all aspects of healthcare. This led the IOM Committee on Patient Safety to conclude in 2003 that "establishing this information technology infrastructure [NHII] should be the highest priority for all health care stakeholders."[10]

In response to the 2001 NCVHS report, HHS began to focus on this issue by adopting health information standards for use by the federal government and licensing the controlled vocabulary, the Systematized Nomenclature of Medicine (SNOMED), for use at no charge by anyone in the U.S. In 2003, the first NHII conference developed a consensus national action agenda.[11] The following year, the President created the Office of the National Coordinator for Health Information Technology (ONC) in HHS and a strategic framework was announced espousing the goals of: (1) informing clinicians; (2) interconnecting clinicians; (3) personalizing care; and (4) improving population health.[12] A public-private collaborative known as *Connecting for Health* has also been actively involved in these issues and continues to both issue reports and recommendations and fund pilot projects.[13] Besides improving safety and quality, it has been estimated that the annual national savings from establishing the NHII could exceed $130 billion, about 8 percent of current healthcare spending.[14] In Washington, DC, a remarkable bipartisan consensus has emerged in support of the need for NHII, leading to joint statements and appearances by such unlikely collaborators as former Speaker of the House Newt Gingrich (R-GA) and U.S. Senator Hillary Clinton (D-NY).

IMPLEMENTATIONS OF ELECTRONIC MEDICAL RECORD SYSTEMS

Due to the cost and complexity of EMR systems, most of the initial deployments have been in large IDNs and academic medical centers. Using these clinical healthcare software systems facilitated legible electronic patient information to be simultaneously available throughout the entire organization, thereby enabling improved patient safety as well as continuity and quality of care, at least within the organization. As these systems were deployed, increasingly complex clinical data was being captured and stored in the organizations' databases. This data could be used for practice management, business intelligence and quality reporting.

EVOLVING PERSONAL HEALTH RECORDS

From the early days of the Internet, there have been many online ePHR offerings. However, almost all of these have required that the consumer enter and maintain all of the data in the record. Frustrating for the consumer was the fact that these records did not go anywhere; they were not connected to their doctors' offices. In order for the consumer's data entry work to reach their clinician, the records would have to be printed and brought to the physician. Entrepreneurial health-related Internet sites offered health risk assessment (HRA) tools to the public and sold subscriptions to online behavioral change management resources to assist subscribers in achieving a specific health-related goal such as weight loss or smoking cessation; however, these were standalone applications.

TETHERED PERSONAL HEALTH RECORDS

The providers that had deployed complex electronic systems were able to offer a different model. Once these systems were deployed and a patient could be electronically identified and associated with all of their clinical data in the database, the organizations recognized that further efficiencies could be realized by shifting services and communications directly to the patient through a "tethered" PHR. A tethered ePHR contains data from the single organization that provides the ePHR.

Many of the existing ePHRs are tethered—the patient could be identified by the organization where they were an established patient through the organization's master patient index. Data and services could be provided then to the patient in a HIPAA-compliant private and secure fashion through the tethered ePHR. Once the patient was identified and matched up with his or her data held in the organizations' database, views of this information could be offered to the patient online through any Web browser. The database served as the two-way mirror reflecting the same data to clinicians within the organization and selected portions of that data to the patients that were treated within the organization. These tethered PHRs have functioned as important tools to encourage consumer compliance with medical regimens including primary and secondary preventative medicine and chronic condition management. In this context, primary prevention means assisting individuals from developing a disease; secondary prevention includes activities aimed at early disease detection to cure or prevent progression of the disease; and chronic condition management is a form of secondary prevention that endeavors to decrease individuals' morbidity from a disease that they have already acquired.

These systems could also provide a variety of services such as prescription renewal, appointment scheduling and secure messaging between the patient and provider(s) given that they are directly linked to the clinical system deployed throughout the healthcare organization and, in most instances, provided by the same software vendor. As the systems become more sophisticated, they include added functionality and tools such as the ability for patients to enter data online for their doctors to receive directly through the clinical software systems, thereby enhancing the physician-patient relationship and improving the quality of care.

In this environment, an individual who receives care from unrelated providers offering tethered ePHRs might well have multiple separate ePHRs that they are obliged to utilize if they want to become involved in managing their healthcare. A consumer who is responsible for the care of a loved one as a proxy caregiver may also need to be enrolled in additional separate systems to manage their care. The examples above underscore the disconnected flow and storage of electronic health information throughout the healthcare industry and all of its constituents. Even if there were federal mandates for individuals to have electronic access to their health information, there is no single source of this information in the current state. Retrieving the accumulated information would require accessing multiple disparate sources. This environment renders the prospect of consumer health management difficult for even the most sophisticated healthcare consumers.

Clearly, the easiest arrangement for the consumer is to receive all of their care within a single provider organization given that the provider organization is financially unmotivated to share the information electronically with other provider organizations or to make this information available to the consumer in an electronically transportable fashion.

PAYOR-BASED PERSONAL HEALTH RECORDS

The initial electronic systems used in healthcare were billing systems. Arguably the current most complete health-related information for an individual resides within payors' electronic systems from their claims data. Payor information includes results, medications and provider encounters. Payors such as Aetna, United Healthcare, and others have also been developing tethered ePHRs based on their electronic claims data coming from a variety of healthcare constituent electronic systems, including providers, pharmacies, laboratories and others. These ePHR systems are financed by the payors and provided to their insured. Some of these payors offer ePHRs in an effort to achieve the goals of decreasing healthcare costs through primary and secondary prevention as well as chronic condition management. Several payors have developed licensed ePHRs that include chronic care and preventive medicine algorithms. These systems scan an individual's claims data relative to the algorithms developed and then send alerts to the individual if they are due or overdue for a test. Such systems have been termed "sentinel" intervention systems.

A 2005 study of the use of a sentinel system describes the system developed as, "…a clinical decision support system that uses the clinical information contained in administrative claims data from physicians, hospitals, pharmacies, and clinical laboratories to identify common errors in care and departures from widely accepted clinical guidelines. Therefore, the system can operate in any fee-for-service clinical environment or other environment in which encounter data are reported without requiring any cooperation from the caregiver community beyond responding to clinical recommendations as they are issued. Because of its ongoing vigilance in monitoring patient information … we applied the term *sentinel system* to distinguish its function from point-of-care decision support."[15] In one study, the sentinel system developed was designed to relay the recommendations to the treating clinicians, rather than directly to the patients. The authors concluded that the use of the system, "…was associated with a reduction in hospitalization, medical costs, and morbidity."[15]

As the data in the payors' electronic systems comes from multiple sources, it may be more complete than data within the healthcare organization's system. For example, in the ambulatory care environment, if a physician has prescribed a medication and a laboratory test for a patient for a given condition, the provider's electronic clinical system will record the ordering data. However, if the patient fills the prescription and has the test performed outside the clinician's healthcare organization, the clinician's system will not have the information regarding whether or not the patient has filled (and eventually refilled) the prescription or if the patient had the test and what was the test result. For the provider's electronic clinical system to have this information in its database, an interoperable environment between healthcare constituents with its inherent technical and administrative complexities would be required. The payor's electronic system, however, would at least be aware of whether or not the patient had filled the prescription and completed the test, based on the payor's claims data. But their systems might not include other pertinent clinical data (e.g., allergies, vital signs and physical exam findings). The payor system would obviously not include medications, tests or treatments that the patient had paid for out of pocket.

Branches of the U.S. government that are payors, including the U.S. Department of Veterans Affairs (VA) and CMS, have also invested in ePHR initiatives. According to the VA, its ePHR, My HealtheVet (MHV), "…is the gateway to veteran health benefits and services. It provides access to: trusted health information, links to federal and VA benefits and resources, the Personal Health Journal, online VA prescription refill. In the future, MHV registrants will be able to view appointments, copay balances, and key portions of their VA medical records online."[16]

CMS offers MyMedicare.gov, which is a "…free, secure online service for accessing your Medicare information."[17] In addition, in 2007, CMS announced that they are "…partnering with a group of health plans for a program designed to encourage Medicare beneficiaries to use PHRs…the new program, whose participants include HIP USA, Humana, Kaiser Permanente and the University of Pittsburgh Medical Center, hopes to boost the level of consumer PHR use."[18]

Other healthcare constituents such as employers or benefit funds have also decided to develop ePHRs. One such example is Dossia.* According to Dossia's Web site, the organization hosts "… an independent and secure Web-based system that will enable participating employees, their dependents and retirees to maintain

---

* Note: Author Dr. Holly Miller serves on the Dossia Physicians Advisory Board.

lifelong electronic health records. The Dossia system will empower individuals to gather their own medical data from multiple sources and to create and utilize their own personal, private and portable electronic health record. In the beginning, data is likely to come from insurers' databases and the patient's own annotations. As the system develops, additional information will come directly from the patient's medical chart. At first these records will be offered only to employees and dependents of the founder companies. Because Dossia is independently owned and operated, employers and insurance companies will have no access to any information in any employee's health record. In the future, as users change jobs or insurance companies or retire, they will retain access to Dossia."[19]

EMPLOYER-OFFERED PERSONAL HEALTH RECORDS

The employers that have come together to build and support Dossia include companies such as Intel, AT&T and Wal-Mart. This system is an effort to begin to construct a transportable ePHR that attempts to aggregate an individual's electronic health information. This is an extremely complex task for two reasons. First, aggregating data from providers would mean building and maintaining interfaces to an ever-growing number of providers that have implemented diverse EMR systems. Second, the majority of providers are still maintaining paper records and do not have their patient data available electronically. It appears that the first attempts to collect such electronic information will come from insurer systems' electronic claims data as "…connecting with EMRs is actually a low priority because too few doctors use them. Dossia will start by collecting data from the Electronic Claims Clearing House, where health care providers file insurance claims. Such 'raw' data is more informative than what insurers would provide."[20]

MICROSOFT® AND GOOGLE™

Microsoft® entered the PHR arena with HealthVault™, and Google™ with Google™ Health. Though not itself an ePHR, HealthVault is a Web-based infrastructure to support ePHR data from a variety of ePHR applications. Microsoft launched the HealthVault site on October 4, 2007, with the following functions: HealthVault Search—

to search the Web for healthcare articles and health information; HealthVault Account—a platform to support the consumer-directed accumulation of aggregated personal health information where the healthcare consumer controls their health information therein; and HealthVault Connection Center—to "connect a wide variety of HealthVault-compatible devices from partners to your PC and upload the data to your HealthVault account."[21] At the HealthVault announcement, Microsoft also stated that multiple provider and disease prevention organizations will work with them to build upon their technology platform. In contrast, Google offers both a PHR and a platform.

The entrance of Microsoft and Google into the PHR market has enabled the consumer-controlled movement of personal health information. The information can, however, only be moved electronically between providers that are using EMR systems.

This is a potentially transformative innovation. The outstanding question is whether or not consumers will adopt this technology now that it is available.

REFERENCES

1. Institute of Medicine. *The Computer-Based Patient Record: An Essential Technology for Patient Care.* Washington, DC: National Academy Press; 1991.
2. Institute of Medicine. *To Err is Human: Building a Safer Health Care System.* Washington, DC: National Academy Press; 1999.
3. McGlynn EA, Asch SM, Adams, J, et al. The quality of health care delivered to adults in the United States. *NEJM.* 2003; 348:2635-2645.
4. Institute of Medicine. *Crossing the Quality Chasm: A New Health System for the 21st Century.* Washington, DC: National Academy Press; 2001.
5. Institute of Medicine. *Fostering Rapid Advances in Health Care: Learning from System Demonstrations.* Washington, DC: National Academy Press; 2002.
6. President's Information Technology Advisory Committee. Transforming health care through information technology: report to the president, February 2001. Available at: http://www.itrd.gov/pubs/pitac/pitac-hc-9feb01.pdf. Accessed June 12, 2008.
7. President's Information Technology Advisory Committee. Revolutionizing health care through information technology: report to the president, June 2004. Available at http://www.nitrd.gov/pitac/reports/20040721_hit_report.pdf. Accessed June 12, 2008.

8. National Research Council. *Computer Science and Telecommunications Board. Networking Health: Prescriptions for the Internet.* Washington, DC: National Academy Press; 2001.

9. National Committee on Vital and Health Statistics. Information for health: A strategy for building the national health information infrastructure. November 15, 2001. Available at: http://www.ncvhs.hhs.gov/nhiilayo.pdf. Accessed June 12, 2008.

10. Institute of Medicine. *Patient Safety: Achieving a New Standard for Care.* Washington, DC: National Academy Press; 2003.

11. Yasnoff WA, Humphreys BL, Overhage JM, Detmer DE, Brennan PF, Morris RW, Middleton B, Bates DW, Fanning JP. A consensus action agenda for achieving the national health information infrastructure. *J Am Med Informatics Assoc.* 2004; 11(4):332-338.

12. U.S. Department of Health and Human Services. The decade of health information technology: Delivering consumer-centric and information-rich health care, framework for strategic action. July 21, 2004. Available at: http://www.os.dhhs.gov/healthit/documents/hitframework.pdf. Accessed June 12, 2008.

13. Connecting for Health. Achieving electronic connectivity in healthcare: A preliminary roadmap from the nation's public and private-sector healthcare leaders. July 2004. Available at: http://www.connectingforhealth.org/resources/cfh_aech_roadmap_072004.pdf. Accessed June 12, 2008.

14. Pan E, Johnston D, Walker J, Adler-Milstein J, Bates DW, Middleton B. *The Value of Healthcare Information Exchange and Interoperability.* Boston, MA: Center for Information Technology Leadership; 2004.

15. Javitt, et al. Using a claims data-based sentinel system to improve compliance with clinical guidelines: Results of a randomized prospective study. *American Journal of Managed Care.* 2005; 11(2):93-102.

16. My HealtheVet homepage. U.S. Department of Veterans Affairs Web site. Available at: http://www.myhealth.va.gov/. Accessed June 12, 2008.

17. My Medicare homepage. U.S. Health and Human Services Web site. Available at: http://www.mymedicare.gov/. Accessed June 12, 2008.

18. CMS launches PHR program with health plans. *FierceHealthIT Weekly News for Health IT Leaders.* June 24, 2007. Available at: http://www.fiercehealthit.com/story/cms-launches-phr-program-with-health-plans/2007-06-25. Accessed June 12, 2008.

19. Dossia. Frequently asked questions. Available at: http://www.dossia.org/consumers/faq#one. Accessed June 12, 2008.

20. Baker ML. Large employers to provide online personal health records. *eWeek.com.* December 7, 2006, Available at: http://www.eweek.com/article2/0,1895,2069942,00.asp. Accessed June 12, 2008.

21. HealthVault homepage. Microsoft Healthvault Web site. Available at: http://www.healthvault.com/. Accessed June 11, 2008.

CHAPTER 3

Definitions, Models and Functions of ePHRs, PBHRs, EMRs and EHRs

Clearly, there is an enormous amount of money and effort being focused on PHRs. To best develop a PHR model that will truly help to address some of the issues in healthcare previously cited as well as create a system capable of our needed healthcare transformation, let us start with defining several component HIT systems: EMR, EHR, and PHR.

Their definitions, along with Payor Based Health Records (PBHRs), continue to be in flux and it is difficult to point to a single universally accepted agreement for definitions for any of these terms. In October, 2007, the National Alliance for Health Information Technology (NAHIT)[1] launched a request for organizations to submit definitions for the following terms: EHR, EMR, PHR, health information exchange (HIE) and regional health information organization (RHIO).

The organization offered the following rationale from their Web site, "A cacophony of competing and confusing definitions, with terms often used interchangeably, is impeding progress in health information technology. A common understanding and use of terms are essential for facilitating IT adoption and innovation and achieving a useful exchange of health information to improve patient outcomes... Our task is to sort through the similarities and differences in the definitions, look for concept and language commonalities and to do an attribute comparison in order to ultimately begin to standardize health information technology terms."[2]

For the purposes of this book, we will attempt to define an EMR, PHR, PBHR and EHR. We will also reference an analysis of the commonalities and differences of several of the original PHR definitions that have been submitted by HIMSS, the American Medical Informatics Association (AMIA) and the Markle Foundation.

ELECTRONIC MEDICAL RECORD (EMR)

The NAHIT EMR definition is "an electronic record of health-related information on an individual that can be created, gathered, managed, and consulted by authorized clinicians and staff within one health care organization."[3]

The features and functions may vary somewhat, but generally they include the following capabilities: clinical documentation, results review and management, patient lists or scheduled patients, physician order entry, best practice alerts and clinical messaging. To be useful, the information in the EMR should reflect all aspects of the course of care, what information was available at what point in the care process, what the provider was thinking and what the provider did. The information must be maintained in a secure manner that protects the privacy of the information contained therein. The EMR must satisfy HIPAA requirements, and must include, at a minimum, those elements necessary to satisfy the state law as well as Medicare and Medicaid program participation under federal and state law for a legal medical record. State law requirements are addressed in Chapter 8 more completely; but, in summary, providers are required to maintain records (over a number of years) that contain the information gathered from the patient (history and physical), about the patient (clinical and diagnostic tests), diagnoses, prescriptions and treatments. It is an impractical exercise to pretend that some components of an EMR would be segregated for legal medical records purposes. The powers of state and federal governments and the discovery rules for courts would make all other material available in any case.

The EMR may contain, and in more sophisticated models does contain, additional functionalities to enhance the provider's ability to provide care. Such functionalities will include clinical features to improve care, quality and safety. One such feature might be e-prescribing and best practice drug-drug interaction alerts prior to e-signing a new prescription. Another feature might be direct secure Web-based communication with patients through an EMR system tethered ePHR. Some EMRs also include functions for utilizing the information for secondary purposes such as reporting/data retrieval, quality of care, practice management, research, practice efficiencies and interfaces to other internal systems like billing.

Just as the "Good Housekeeping Seal of Approval" is a recognized statement regarding the *Good Housekeeping* magazine's Consumer's Policy that backs up consumer products with the seal, the Certification Commission for Healthcare Information Technology (CCHIT) functions to certify health information technology products. CCHIT is a "recognized certification body (RCB) for electronic health records and their networks, and an independent, voluntary, private-sector initiative."[4] The CCHIT mission is to accelerate the adoption of HIT by creating an efficient, credible and sustainable certification program. The organization was formed in 2004 and it "...was awarded [in 2005] a contract by the U.S. Department of Health and Human Services (HHS) to develop, create prototypes for, and evaluate the certification criteria and inspection process for electronic health records (EHRs)."[4]

Commercial EMRs are licensed from an EMR vendor and financed by the provider organization. They are distributed to affiliated providers with provider access being role-based. Some large IDNs or academic medical centers have developed their own EMRs where the EMR is owned and the development is financed by the provider organization.

The development of EHRs, discussed below, may well lead to a need for change in the laws governing legal medical records, because the need to store all patient information is obviated by its availability elsewhere. Moreover, one important and unanswered question for providers is the extent that they are responsible for accessing relevant information that is universally and instantaneously available now or in the future.

PAYOR-BASED HEALTH RECORDS (PBHR)

Arguably, the broadest source of currently available digitized patient health information is collected and stored by payors in their claims systems. Payors, in the course of making utilization, coverage, care management, disease management and payment decisions, have extensive digital files containing health insurance claims information across providers for each covered health plan member.

Many payors make some aspect of the PBHR available to providers and patients. Some payors offer ePHRs sourced from the PBHRs through their member portals and some make a version of the PBHR available directly to providers for use at the point-of-care. Whatever depth the PBHR may lack, today in many cases it provides the broadest possible view of a patient's care.

ELECTRONIC PERSONAL HEALTH RECORDS (PHR, OR ePHR)

The PHR as defined by the Key Health Information Technology Terms Project is: "[a]n electronic, record of health related information on an individual that conforms to nationally recognized interoperability standards and that can be drawn from multiple sources while being managed, shared, and controlled by the individual."[5]

HIMSS defines an ePHR in its ePHR Definition and Position Statement by stating, "An electronic Personal Health Record ("ePHR") is a universally accessible, layperson comprehensible, lifelong tool for managing relevant health information, promoting health maintenance and assisting with chronic disease management via an interactive, common data set of electronic health information and e-health tools. The ePHR is controlled, managed, and shared by the individual or his or her legal proxy(s) and must be secure to protect the privacy and confidentiality of the health information it contains. It is not a legal record unless so defined and is subject to various legal limitations."[6]

It is the healthcare consumer's view of this data with management tools that allow for the determination of access and data distribution for their direct clinical care as well as for secondary uses of their data. The primary purpose of the ePHR is to empower individual healthcare consumers to interact with the healthcare system and work with tools provided within the ePHR to achieve their personal best possible health and wellness outcomes, chronic care management, and enhance the health and wellness of the community and of the nation. To this end, data should be directly and automatically "pushed" into the ePHR from all of the healthcare constituents that have data pertaining to the individual. Individuals should not be required to go to all of the constituents to request their data or to have to "pull" their data into the ePHR.

Having data and information interfaced from all healthcare constituents would allow the healthcare consumer to seamlessly manage all aspects of their health and wellness. Consumers could have the immediate benefit of a direct link to their primary care provider (or their "medical home") as well as the tools, links and electronic flow of information to manage every aspect of their health.

The essential concept of the "medical home" is that patient-centered care requires coordination across the continuum, beyond a given acute care episode, with the identification of necessary medical and community resources that will meet the individual's care needs. A key element in support of the medical home is HIT, specifically ePHRs. In March, 2007, the American Academy of Family Physicians (AAFP), American Academy of Pediatrics (AAP), American College of Physicians (ACP) and the American Osteopathic Association (AOA) joined together to develop the Joint Principles of the Patient-Centered Medical Home. These essential principles are: a personal physician; physician directed medical practice; whole person orientation; coordinated and/or integrated care; and quality, safety, access and payment enhancements.[7]

Ultimately, consumers could potentially connect through their ePHR to a self-selected community that either shares the same health-related interests or wants to achieve health-related behavioral goals. From the same system, an individual could someday:

- Be reminded of any health maintenance requirements for themselves or their loved ones based on personalized protocols developed from population study algorithms.
- Be nagged by their weight loss and exercise partner that they had not documented in the system their weight or exercise in the last two days.
- Receive a system-generated alert that the information from their home bathroom scale indicated a three-pound weight gain in the last week.
- Request a prescription refill from the pharmacy or a renewal from their doctor, and be informed when the prescription is ready for pick up at the pharmacy.
- Be informed that their mother has not been taking her medicine and discuss this electronically with their mother's doctor.
- Be reminded that one of their children is due for his annual physical, and that another is due to have her medications refilled.
- Observe how their smoking cessation success will affect their lifetime morbidity and mortality as well as its financial impact on their lives.
- Compare healthcare insurance plans.
- Pay their copays.
- Complete a pre-visit questionnaire that will be "pushed" directly to the doctor, and used in the doctor's EMR as the basis for part of the doctor's clinical documentation for the visit.
- Analyze provider quality, outcome and cost data to select the best local, national or international provider for required tertiary care; then schedule an appointment; and release all or selected portions of their medical information to the provider to view.

There are some fundamental elements of the ePHR that include considerations of enabling features and functions, including patient-centered e-health tools; interoperability and information exchange; and privacy and security. Although e-health tools would be useful to many consumers, a PHR without a full set of such tools would still be useful. In fact, at times less information can be more useful than an information overload.

ePHR Features, Functions, Consumer Tools and Information Links

- The ePHR interfaces to all other pertinent health and wellness information that applies to the healthcare consumer, including:
    - ❑ All provider quality, outcomes and cost transparency data;
    - ❑ The consumers' healthcare insurance information and health savings account information, if applicable;
    - ❑ Comparative healthcare insurer plan benefits information
    - ❑ All pertinent healthcare billing systems;
    - ❑ Personal wellness, health maintenance and chronic disease management tools;
    - ❑ Community-based wellness, health maintenance and chronic disease management tools;
    - ❑ Behavioral data entry tools such as food and/or activity diaries
    - ❑ Genetic data, if available;
    - ❑ Extensive tailored, consumer friendly health information and health information search tools;
    - ❑ Information about relevant clinical trials and clinical trial search tools;
    - ❑ Ability to select to receive regional or national diagnosis code-based clinical trial information;
    - ❑ Pharmacy interfaces to request prescription renewals;
    - ❑ Interactive communication tools with the consumer's healthcare provider(s) such as messaging, appointment scheduling, prescription renewal, etc.;
    - ❑ Interfaces to all pertinent clinical data including all results, procedures, diagnoses and histories;
    - ❑ The consumer's personal standalone or implanted medical device data such as pacemaker, pedometer or glucometer data; and
    - ❑ Alerts and reminders tailored to the healthcare consumer that would be triggered by interfaced "sentinel systems" as developed by provider, payor or other healthcare constituents using an electronic system.

Technical

- The ePHR is both information contained in a repository and a portal to external health information. It is interoperable such that the information contained is freely e-transportable, designed to move with the patient and to be a lifetime health record.

Privacy and Security

- Data, as discussed above, is distributed based on the decision of the ePHR owner or their proxy. Responsibility for these decisions as well as their potential consequences and benefits would need to be clearly identified in layperson-friendly terms within the ePHR.

TETHERED "ePHR"

As previously described, this term refers to the patient's view of a single source of data (for example, data from a healthcare provider organization's EMR or the data from a payor organization). These systems frequently have both healthcare and practice efficiency related tools such as bill paying, appointment requests, and health maintenance or chronic disease management reminders and other tools. These systems are not inherently comprehensive or transportable.

It should be noted that at the present time the ePHR likely to have the most complete healthcare data for the individual is the payor-based ePHR, as the payor receives all of the individual's aggregated claims data. These systems do not include clinical data from the provider EMRs or services or treatments paid for out of pocket, but do include the billing data for provider encounters, filled prescriptions and completed tests or studies.

In addition, both HealthVault and Google are interested in interfacing to these tethered ePHRs and storing aggregated patient data on their Web servers, potentially making that data transportable and interoperable across the tethered ePHRs that have interfaced to a third party Web server.

CURRENT PHR MODELS

The PHR market continues to rapidly change and grow. There are many sources and models of PHRs currently in use which are provided by a variety of healthcare constituents.

The CCHIT Personal Health Records Task Force wanted to anticipate the evolving PHR market in their certification advice. Their recommendations included, "…with the PHR market still evolving, certification should create a "big tent" that can accommodate a diversity of models and architectures for delivering personal health information to consumers…[C]ertification should be simple for consumers to understand, offering them a "safety zone" where they could be comfortable that their information was private and secure,…[and] that the PHR Work Group and the Commission's Interoperability Work Group collaborate to develop criteria that will ensure that PHRs can send and receive data from as many potential sources as possible, such as ambulatory EHRs, hospital EHRs, payers, pharmacies and labs."[8]

Figure 3-1 demonstrates the current evolving landscape of PHRs and the desired interoperability between these elements. The diagram distinguishes PHR applications, PHR platforms, and Health Information Data Sources.

Figure 3-1: Diverse PHR Models for Certification

(Reprinted with permission from the Certification Commission for Healthcare Information Technology. Copyright © 2008.)

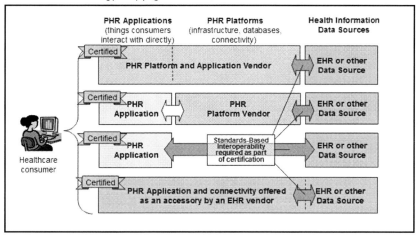

ELECTRONIC HEALTH RECORD (EHR)

The EHR is the aggregated and rationalized source of information from all available healthcare constituent sources, including, but not limited to, EMRs, PBHRs, and ePHRs.

The EHR as defined by the Key Health Information Technology Terms Project is: "an electronic record of health-related information on an individual that conforms to nationally recognized interoperability standards and that can be created, managed, and consulted by authorized clinicians and staff across more than one health care organization."[9]

In October 2006, the HIMSS Electronic Health Record Vendors Association (EHRVA) defined an EHR as "…a longitudinal electronic record of patient health information produced by encounters in one or more care settings. Included in this information are patient demographics, progress notes, problems, medications, vital signs, past medical history, immunizations, laboratory data and radiology reports. The EHR automates and streamlines the clinician's workflow. The EHR has the ability to independently generate a complete record of a clinical patient encounter, as well as supporting other care-related activities such as decision support, quality management, and clinical reporting."[10]

An EHR is:

- An interoperable, shared system that supports and enhances care at its delivery point as well as supporting all of the proposed secondary purposes of the data gathered, including improved quality, safety and continuity of care.
- A reporting/data retrieval system for the purposes of care management that can be segmented so that it is only available to the provider organization generating the data. Data retrieval for the purposes of quality or other required reporting could be readily made available to the necessary reporting agencies across all providers in the interoperable EHR exchange, thereby greatly decreasing the costs to each individual organization or group.
- A best practices distribution tool as data from a specific healthcare constituent that has achieved practice efficiencies, improved quality or decreased healthcare costs might be shared throughout

the community served by the interoperable EHR for the benefit of solving the healthcare issues in our nation.

The NAHIT Defining Key Health Information Technology Terms project reported "[the] distinction between records according to their ability to exchange information interoperably is the principal difference between an EHR, which can exchange information interoperably, and an EMR which cannot." The same report identifies the differences between an EHR and a PHR as "...in a PHR, access to the record must be managed and controlled by the individual. Information that passes from an EHR to a PHR transfers to the control of the individual."

Optimally, a truly interoperable EHR could ultimately capture data pertaining to consumer demographics, clinical, behavioral (as entered by the individual), genetic, pharmacy, results, medical devices, etc. Analysis of the aggregated de-identified data from large populations using such a rich database could allow researchers to create predictive models. These models could be used for a multitude of purposes, including appropriately allocating healthcare resources, developing personalized medicine and creating targeted individual-focused behavioral change support programs. The predictive models resulting from the analysis of the information from large population studies could enable providers to truly personalize medicine. Practicing personalized medicine, a clinician could select the single medication for a patient with a given condition that would be the most effective with the lowest side effects profile or predict that an individual is susceptible for a given condition and take steps to prevent it with targeted clinical or behavioral interventions.

For example, not everyone who is obese develops diabetes and heart disease; if susceptible individuals could be identified, they could enroll in targeted behavioral and clinical intervention programs. Using the predictive models based on behavioral contribution to disease, it would be possible to demonstrate to healthcare consumers the impact of their current behaviors on their health and then provide individual-based tools through a PHR to support behavioral change. Data analyses for research purposes could have a major impact not only on transformative research projects, but also on the speed to which significant discoveries could be incorporated into evidence-based standards of medical care.

In addition, aggregated population data could be analyzed to predict and plan for the care needs of populations. Such planning would include the management of chronic care populations as well as the development of predictive models to create targeted preventive measures for specific populations at risk.

One of the shortcomings in achieving the level of interoperability and data integration across HIT systems required for the proposed ideal models of EHRs and ePHRs is the current lack of an international standard healthcare data model. With an increased emphasis on the ability to capture, reuse and exchange discrete data across HIT systems for clinical and secondary purposes (such as research or reporting), the lack of a healthcare data standard that transverses HIT systems is a barrier to achieving this goal. This is both an obstacle within and certainly across healthcare constituent organizations. Without more comprehensive use of healthcare data standards, HIT system developers will continue to use or create unique or proprietary data models that make the processes of interoperability of discrete data exchange more difficult.

There are groups working to create international standards; however, none have been universally adopted in HIT to date. The International Organization for Standardization (ISO) is a non-governmental organization including representatives from many national standards organizations. Founded in 1947, it is dedicated to developing and promoting international industrial and commercial standards. According to its Web site, "ISO has more than 16,500 International Standards and other types of normative documents in its current portfolio. ISO's work program ranges from standards for traditional activities such as agriculture and construction, through mechanical engineering, manufacturing and distribution, to transport, medical devices, information and communication technologies, and to standards for good management practice and for services." The organization's scope includes "standardization in the field of information for health, and Health Information and Communications Technology (ICT) to achieve compatibility and interoperability between independent systems. Also, [ISO strives] to ensure compatibility of data for comparative statistical purposes (e.g., classifications), and to reduce duplication of effort and redundancies."[11]

The adoption of an international HIT data model would also facilitate the process of data normalization or canonical synthesis (i.e., the process of designing relational databases to ensure data integrity) and metadata tagging to improve data retrieval and system performance. Ultimately, enormous cost savings could be introduced to HIT and, thereby to healthcare, if a more comprehensive HIT data standard could be developed that would facilitate interoperability.

Another issue that might be an impediment to the realization of true EHRs is the issue of data ownership. Some healthcare constituents consider the health information in their systems to be proprietary. Healthcare constituents might use their aggregated data for a variety of secondary purposes including business reporting, research or sales to other healthcare constituents such as the pharmaceutical industry. Recently, individuals have been wondering what authority they have over the secondary use of their data; questions of the ability for individuals to be able to opt in or out to secondary uses of their data and data ownership have been raised.

CONCLUSION

Recognizing common definitions of many frequently used HIT terms is in process. However, as technology continues to evolve, the terms and what they define will need to change as well. In trying to identify a current definition of an ePHR, the common elements across several HIT organizations have included:

- Privacy and security;
- Lifelong records;
- Control by the healthcare consumer or their proxy, including any secondary uses of the data;
- The ability to be universally accessible and transportable; and
- The containment of all the necessary tools, features and functions for a healthcare consumer to best manage their health, wellness and behaviors.

Despite the growth of ePHR offerings throughout the marketplace in the last several years, it has been interesting to note that most ePHRs actively being used appear to be tethered to a provider, insurer or other healthcare constituency group. Most of the interoperable EHRs that have been developed to date (both those with shared databases in a centralized model or those with separate linked databases in a federated model) have not focused on the ePHR being a fundamental element of the design or for the data flow to be managed and shared by the healthcare consumer. Rather, they focus on complex rules defined by the participating provider organizations. Healthcare consumers are beginning to realize the value of the PHR and may very soon be seeking PHRs as defined above. In fact, there are efforts underway by a variety of organizations such as the American Health Information Management Association (AHIMA) to educate the public regarding ePHRs.

An ePHR that would meet the needs of the provider, consumer and other healthcare constituents could be based on a centralized repository or "platform" that included, or was interfaced to, all healthcare constituents' data. A uniform data model would facilitate system performance and the ability to integrate data from one constituent's system to another. The model would support pushing pertinent data to the end user, rather than the user needing to pull the data to them. This would enhance the workflow of the system users. All such integrated data would be tagged with its original source and data and time stamped. Data movement could be controlled by the individual to whom the data pertains. Data from a given healthcare constituent's HIT system could be partitioned to protect their business interests; however, the comprehensive data necessary for the constituents' clinical or business needs would be readily and immediately available.

Beyond data movement as regulated by HIPAA, all secondary uses of data could be controlled by the individual to whom the data pertains. Such a model might ultimately have an impact on the provision of individual-centered care across the continuum and the concept of a medical home. Ultimately, it could enhance care efficiency and decrease healthcare costs.

REFERENCES

1. NAHIT homepage. National Alliance for Health Information Technology Web site. Available at: www.nahit.org. Accessed June 12, 2008.
2. NAIIIT. Reaching consensus: Defining key health information technology terms. Available at: http://definitions.nahit.org/definitions.php. Accessed June 12, 2008.

3. The National Alliance for Health Information Technology. Defining Key Health Information Technology Terms. April 28, 2008. Available at: http://definitions. nahit.org/doc/HITTermsFinalReport_508v2.pdf.

4. CCHIT homepage. Certification Commission for Healthcare Information Technology Web site. Available at: http://www.cchit.org/about/index.asp. Accessed June 12, 2008.

5. The National Alliance for Health Information Technology. Defining Key Health Information Technology Terms. April 28, 2008. Available at: http://definitions. nahit.org/doc/HITTermsFinalReport_508v2.pdf. (Note that the HIMSS definition and those of other organizations are discussed and compared in a chart in the Appendix to this chapter.)

6. HIMSS ePHR Definition and Position Statement. (A full copy of this statement is available in Appendix B.)

7. Joint Principles of the Patient-Centered Medical Home. March, 2007. http:// www.medicalhomeinfo.org/Joint%20Statement.pdf.

8. Reber S, Koziol W. Patient Privacy Focus of Task Force on Personal Health Records Certification. *CCHIT News.* Chicago; July 24, 2008.

9. The National Alliance for Health Information Technology. Defining Key Health Information Technology Terms. April 28, 2008. Available at: http://definitions. nahit.org/doc/HITTermsFinalReport_508v2.pdf.

10. HIMSS EHRVA Definitional Model and Application Process. October 2006. http://www.himssehrva.org/docs/EHRVA_application.pdf.

11. ISO homepage. International Organization for Standardization Web site. Available at: http://www.iso.org/iso/home.htm. Accessed June 12, 2008.

APPENDIX

In 2007, HIMSS published a "PHR Definition and Position Statement" which is included in this Appendix.

Several other organizations have published PHR definitions. As part of the submission of the HIMSS' PHR definition to the HIMSS Board of Directors, an analysis between the HIMSS' definition and these existing definitions was undertaken, looking for exact or similar terminology used in the definitions, not necessarily looking for the ideas represented within the definitions. The analysis compared the HIMSS' June, 2007 definition and position statement with the following:

• The Value of Personal Health Records, A Joint Position Statement for Consumers of Health Care by American Health Information Management Association;

• American Medical Informatics Association, February 2007; and

- Connecting Americans to Their Health Care: A Common Framework for Networked Personal Health Information, The Connector for Health Common Framework, The Markle Foundation, December 7, 2006.

The Table 3A-1 represents the results of this analysis. [*]

---

[*] The authors would like to thank JoAnn Klinedinst for this comparative analysis.

Table 3A-1: Draft Comparisons of PHR Definitions across the Industry*

	AHIMA/AMIA	Markle	HIMSS
Comments about PHRs across the Three Organizations			
An Electronic Tool		✓	✓
A PHR Consolidates Medical Information in One Place	✓		✓
PHR is Transparent		✓	✓
Supports the Development of Interoperable ePHRs		✓	✓
Distinct from EHRs		✓	
Universally Accessible	✓	✓	✓
Layperson Comprehensible	✓		✓
Lifelong Tool for Managing Relevant Health Information	✓	✓	✓
Intended to Serve the Public		✓	
A PHR May Be Tethered/Connected		✓	✓
A PHR May Be Untethered/Standalone		✓	✓
PHR Platforms		✓	
Web-based		✓	
PC		✓	
Portable Device		✓	
USB Keys		✓	
Mobile Phones		✓	
Smart Cards		✓	
Implantable Devices		✓	
PHR Sponsors		✓	
Employers		✓	
Heathcare Providers		✓	
Insurance Plans		✓	
Pharmacy Services		✓	
Affinity Groups		✓	
Dot-coms		✓	
Device Makers		✓	
Disease Management Companies		✓	
Search Engines		✓	
Business Model		✓	

continued

Draft Comparisons of PHR Definitions across the Industry*

	AHIMA/AMIA	Markle	HIMSS
Comments about PHRs across the Three Organizations			
An Electronic Tool		✓	✓
Licensing Fees		✓	
Services/Transaction Fees		✓	
Advertisements		✓	
Subscription Fees		✓	
Value Proposition		✓	
Loyalty and Marketing		✓	
Process Efficiency		✓	
Messaging		✓	
Behavior and Outcomes		✓	
Health Information is Controlled by the Individual/Proxy		✓	
Health Information is Owned by the Individual/Proxy	✓		✓
Health Information is Managed by the Individual/Proxy	✓		✓
Health Information is Shared by the Individual/Proxy	✓		✓
Sources of Data		✓	✓
Consumer-Sourced Data		✓	✓
Professionally-Sourced Data		✓	✓
Device-Sourced Data		✓	✓
Receives Data from all Constituents that Participate in Individual's Healthcare	✓		✓
Allows Individual/Proxy to Enter Their Own Data	✓		✓
Allows Individual/Proxy to Designate Read-Only Access to the ePHR			✓
Provides for Unique Patient Identification			✓
Allows Secure Access to Information	✓	✓	✓
Permits the Receipt of Email Alerts			✓
Allows an Individual's Proxy to Act on Behalf of Patient			✓
Provide Technical Support to Constituents at all Times			✓
Champions the Development of National Standards to Ease Burdens Due to Variations in State Laws	✓		✓
Champions the Development of National Standards to Address Legal Concerns	✓		✓

continued

Draft Comparisons of PHR Definitions across the Industry*

	AHIMA/AMIA	Markle	HIMSS
Comments about PHRs across the Three Organizations			
An Electronic Tool		✓	✓
Encourages the Adoption of Incentives			✓
Promotes Health Maintenance			✓
Assists with Chronic Disease Management			✓
Interface is Interative			✓
Secured to Protect the Privacy and Confidentiality of the Health Information	✓	✓	✓
Not a Legal Record	✓	✓	✓
Subject to Various Legal Limitations			✓
Technology Providers Have a Responsibility to Clearly Define Functionality			✓
Individual/Proxy Has a Responsibility to Understand Functionality			✓
Data Can be Imported from Other Applications			✓
Individual/Proxy Can Export Data Out of an ePHR			✓
Adherence to Current and Future Privacy and Security Methods and Standards	✓		✓
PHI Supplied will not be Used for Purposes Other than its Intention (Secondary Use of Data)	✓		✓
Receive Email Alerts			✓
Provides an Audit Trail of all Information Accessed			✓
Access the Privacy Policy of the Source or Offerer of the ePHR	✓		✓
Addresses Administrative, Physical, and Technical Safeguards			✓
Common/Uniform/Minimum Data Set	✓		✓
Personal Identifer	✓	...	✓
Clinical Summary			✓
Active Prescribed Medications	✓		✓
Historical Prescribed Medications			✓
Other Current Non-Prescribed Medications			✓
Allergy Information	✓		✓
Diagnoses/Problem List	✓		✓
Immunization Status	✓		✓

continued

Draft Comparisons of PHR Definitions across the Industry*

	AHIMA/AMIA	Markle	HIMSS
Comments about PHRs across the Three Organizations			
An Electronic Tool		✓	✓
Sensitivities to Drugs or Materials	✓		
Important Test Results	✓		✓
Eye/Dental Records	✓		✓
Results/Reports			✓
Correspondence Between an Individual and His/Her Provider	✓		✓
Contains Information from All Healthcare Providers		✓	✓
Histories			✓
Immunization History			✓
Past Medical History	✓		✓
Surgical History	✓		✓
Family History	✓		✓
Social History			✓
Opinions of Specialists	✓		
Results from a Recent Physicial Examination	✓		✓
Contact and Registration Information	✓		✓
Current Address Information	✓		✓
Current Guarantor Information	✓		✓
Emergency Contact(s)	✓		✓
Primary Care Physician	✓		✓
Other Providers of Care	✓		✓
Current and Historical Insurance Information	✓		✓
Living Wills	✓		✓
Advance Directives	✓		✓
Medical Power of Attorney	✓		✓
Organ Donor Authorization	✓		
Integrated eHealth Tools	✓		✓
Provides Technical Support by Telephone			✓
Provides 24 X 7 Technical Support by Telepone			✓
Ability to Incorporate Patient-Entered Data into their Provider's Legal Medical Record	✓		✓

continued

Draft Comparisons of PHR Definitions across the Industry*

	AHIMA/AMIA	Markle	HIMSS
Comments about PHRs across the Three Organizations			
An Electronic Tool		✓	✓
Supports the Adoption of Incentives by All Constituents			✓
Supports eVisit Billing for ePHR Encounters by Physicians			✓
Empowers Healthcare Consumers to Manage their Health	✓	✓	✓
Empowers Healthcare Consumers to Improve their Health			✓
Empowers Healthcare Consumers to Positively Influence Behavioral Decisions			✓
Empowers Healthcare Consumers to Create a Sense of Partnership with Providers		✓	✓
Ultimately Lowers Healthcare Costs across the United States			✓
Collects Data	✓		
Tracks Data	✓		
Information is Up-to-Date	✓		
Improves Quality of Care	✓		
Effectively Communication with Others about Healthcare	✓		
Data is Accurate	✓		Implied
Data is Reliable	✓		Implied
Data is Complete	✓		Implied
Privacy Protection should follow the PHR	✓		✓
Data must not be used in Discriminatory Practices	✓		
Facilitates Care in an Emergency	✓		
Helps People Prepare for an Appointment	✓		
May Reduce Duplicate Procedures or Processes	✓		

* Prepared for: HIMSS Board of Directors (June 27, 2007)

Despite the appearance of the apparent differences in the definitions as evidenced from Table 3A-1 above, the definitions actually agree on multiple fundamental points:
• Universally accessible;
• Lifelong tool for managing relevant health information;
• Allows secure access to information;
• Secured to protect the privacy and confidentiality of the health information; and
• Empowers healthcare consumers to manage their health.
Of particular note are some of the discrepancies between the definitions. Not all of these definitions agreed that a PHR was electronic, or that the information contained therein needed to be owned, controlled, and

shared by the individual to whom the information referred; however, as stated earlier this did seem to be implied by the organization that omitted this statement.

The following is the HIMSS PHR Definition and Position Statement.

HIMSS Personal Health Records Definition and Position Statement*

Prologue

To enable the goals of reducing medical errors, improving quality of care, and improving the validity of information available to care providers, Personal Health Records (PHRs) function to consolidate an individual's medical information in one place. Recognizing the potential benefits of PHRs, HIMSS works with national consumer-based healthcare organizations to help educate and facilitate the adoption of PHRs. In so doing, HIMSS has taken an active role to facilitate interest in and discussion around this important topic.

PHRs historically have been maintained by individuals in paper form or in unstructured documents on personal computers. More recently, structured *electronic* PHRs (ePHRs) have become available in a variety of formats, and many are Internet-linked with data entered and maintained by the individual or "tethered/connected" to a single specific healthcare, insurance, or other organization that maintains an individual's health records. Some tethered/connected ePHRs are hybrids allowing some information to be entered by the individual. Also, there is an evolution toward interoperable Internet ePHRs that cull all health information relative to the individual who is also responsible for his/her ownership and management.

This document defines an interoperable electronic personal health record, or ePHR, recognizing that this is not the current state of ePHRs but is an appropriate direction for development. It contains guiding principles for ePHR development, and is the work of the HIMSS Personal Health Record Steering Committee and its

---

* The HIMSS Personal Health Records Definition and Position Statement is reproduced with permission of the Healthcare Information and Management Systems Society, 2008.

work groups: Defining the ePHR Work Group and the National ePHR Discussion Work Group.

Statement of Position

HIMSS supports the development of interoperable ePHRs which are interactive and use a common data set of electronic health information and e-health tools. HIMSS envisions ePHRs that are universally accessible and layperson comprehensible, and that may be used as a lifelong tool for managing relevant health information that is owned, managed and shared by the individual or his or her legal proxy(s). The ideal ePHR would receive data from all constituents that participate in the individual's healthcare; allow patients or proxies to enter their own data (such as journals and diaries); and designate read-only access to the ePHR (or designated portions thereof).

HIMSS supports ePHR applications with the following characteristics:
- Provide for unique patient identification;
- Allow secure access to the information contained in the ePHR;
- Permit the receipt of email alerts that do not reveal protected health information (PHI);
- Allow patient proxy(s) to act on behalf of the patient;
- Permit the designation of information to be shared electronically; and,
- Provides technical support to ePHR constituents at all times.

HIMSS champions the development of national standards to ease burdens placed on constituents due to variances in state law and the development of national and uniform state standards to address legal concerns raised by ePHRs such as reliability, reimbursement, ownership, access, transfer, and the limitations, rights and responsibilities of patients and providers for the use of e-health and ePHRs.

Similarly, HIMSS encourages the adoption of incentives by payors, providers, pharmaceutical companies, device manufacturers, and the federal and state governments of the United States to reduce the financial barriers to motivate widespread ePHR adoption.

ePHR Definition

HIMSS defines an ePHR as follows:

> *An electronic Personal Health Record ("ePHR") is a universally accessible, layperson comprehensible, lifelong tool for managing relevant health information, promoting health maintenance and assisting with chronic disease management via an interactive, common data set of electronic health information and e-health tools. The ePHR is owned, managed, and shared by the individual or his or her legal proxy(s) and must be secure to protect the privacy and confidentiality of the health information it contains. It is not a legal record unless so defined and is subject to various legal limitations.*

HIMSS' definition is meant to address the immediate and future developmental direction of ePHRs, with the understanding that any ePHR definition is not static and will evolve with future technology advances and further adoption of electronic health records (EHRs)/ electronic medical records (EMRs) and ePHRs that will create shifts in the culture surrounding the utilization and demand of ePHR constituents.

The ePHR technology providers are encouraged to design applications that meet the needs of the patient; however, technology providers do have a responsibility to clearly define the purpose and intent of how the technology should be used. Likewise, it is the patient's responsibility to understand how the ePHR may function, including, but not limited to, the use and exchange of information in order to exercise one's choice of participating or not participating in a specific ePHR application.

ePHR should include the following characteristics listed by constituency class:

• The individual about whom the ePHR relates:
  □ The proxy(s), or individual(s) who is/are the legally authorized representative(s) of the patient as determined by state law such as a parent or legal guardian if the patient is a minor;
  □ A legal guardian if the patient has been adjudicated incompetent to manage the patient's personal affairs;

- ❏ An agent of the patient authorized under a durable power of attorney for healthcare;
- ❏ An attorney *ad litem* (guardian of the suit) appointed for the patient;
- ❏ A guardian *ad litem* appointed for the patient;
- ❏ A personal representative or statutory beneficiary if the patient is deceased; or
- ❏ An attorney retained by the patient or by another person listed above;
- The healthcare provider or healthcare institution such as hospitals, laboratories, nursing facilities, imaging facilities, pharmacies, physicians, physician groups, nurses, nurse practitioners, and other licensed healthcare professionals, etc.;
- Payors such as individuals, employers, insurers or benefit plans who pay for healthcare; and
- Emergency responders and emergency receivers.

ePHR Models

HIMSS supports ePHR models wherein data within an ePHR can be imported from other applications, (e.g., an EHR/EMR), entered by the patient, or another individual to whom the ePHR owner has granted data entry access, or uploaded from devices. Further, HIMSS supports ePHR models that allow consumers to export data from their ePHR (portability) and allow providers, with patient/proxy consent, to export data out of ePHRs or mine data from ePHRs for legitimately defined purposes such as population health research or health trend analysis.

The current forms of ePHRs in the market mainly involve three basic models:

- Software utilized by individuals to enter and maintain their personal health information;
- Web sites that are maintained by third parties which allow patients to enter and access their information; and
- Web sites that allow patients to view information from other applications such as an institutional EMR/EHR, or from an application that maintains the individual's health insurance claims data.

The latter is referred to as a *tethered/connected* ePHR. These models are not mutually exclusive, and in a tethered/connected model, the patient may have the ability to enter data into the ePHR. Challenges to the adoption of the tethered/connected model depend on the application owner organization.

- In a tethered/connected ePHR model, the ePHR is integrated with another application, such that the application owner organization:
    - ❑ Provides the ePHR to the patient as an electronic portal;
    - ❑ Loads selected PHI into the patient's ePHR;
    - ❑ Provides e-health services via the ePHR; and
    - ❑ Owns and manages the ePHR, allowing patient access.

Note: *The ePHR in this model is not comprehensive and is not a legal medical record.*

If the ePHR is tethered/connected to the EHR/EMR of a provider organization, the challenges to adoption include:

- The current slow adoption of EMRs by medical practices; and
- Provider concerns including:
    - ❑ Sharing of inappropriate information with patients;
    - ❑ Resultant increased workload;
    - ❑ Patient understanding/literacy of the data;
    - ❑ Potential payor contract requirements mandating participation.

If the ePHR is tethered/connected to patient health information applications maintained by insurers or employers, the challenges to adoption include:

- Patient concerns regarding their privacy, and their concerns about such organizations and employers becoming involved in health-related directives rather than such directives coming from their providers.

In an *un-tethered/disconnected* ePHR model, only the patient, or individuals that have been granted access by the patient, has/have the ability to enter PHI into the ePHR.

At present, these models do not support interoperability, allowing patients to freely transfer their self-entered PHI from an un-tethered/connected application to a tethered/connected ePHR, or allowing patients to direct the flow of their PHI between the various applications where it resides including the applications from the various providers where the patient may receive care, and from other organizations involved with their healthcare such as insurers and pharmacies. HIMSS encourages the adoption of ePHRs that support interoperability of common standards and international compatibility.

There are multiple sources from which a consumer may obtain an ePHR such as healthcare providers, employers, health plans, the government, Internet sites, pharmacies, disease management vendors, or device manufacturers, whether tethered/connected or un-tethered/ disconnected. HIMSS champions the development of a universally-accepted ePHR model that would allow patients to:

- Receive data from all constituents that provide or participate in their healthcare;
- Enter their own data (such as journals and diaries);
- Designate read access to the ePHR (either by portion or in its entirety);
- Upload designated portions of their ePHR to interested constituents' electronic systems;
- Provide log of both information shared and information recorded (or entered into the ePHR), including an audit trail of who has entered, accessed, or modified the information; and
- Have access to the privacy policy of the source or offerer of the ePHR.

Privacy, Security and Trust

The HIMSS ePHR definition calls for the adherence to current and future privacy and security methods and standards, as well as addressing the issue of patient "trust" or confidence that the PHI supplied will not be used for purposes other than the intended use (referred to as *secondary use of data*) without the explicit permission of the ePHR owner. To the extent that an entity offering an ePHR is not a covered entity under HIPAA or other privacy and security laws, HIMSS encourages the entity to adopt at a minimum the privacy and security standards of HIPAA as if the organization was a covered entity. HIMSS champions ePHR applications that allow patients to:

- Have unique identification;
- Securely access the system;
- Receive alerts via email that do not contain confidential PHI;

- Provide access to other individual(s) authorized by the patient as a proxy to act on his or her behalf should the need arise;
- Provide an audit trail of all information accessed in the ePHR;
- Designate information to be shared electronically with the patient's consent.
- Access the privacy policy of the source or offerer of the ePHR.

   HIMSS encourages the development of ePHRs that address the most current federal and state privacy and security regulations, including but not limited to, administrative, physical, and technical safeguards. This will enable the clinician/provider of care to comply with laws and regulations that proscribe the circumstances under which PHI may be disclosed without patient authorization. A HIPAA Notice of Privacy Practices must be a part of the ePHR application to enable clinician/provider compliance. Furthermore, to be in compliance with laws and regulations, the ePHR must include standards on secondary uses of patient data.

Common/Uniform/Minimum Data Set

Although there is currently a lack of universal data element standards for ePHRs, HIMSS champions the development of ePHRs with the following minimum data set, which would include an individual's current and historical health and personal information:
- Personal identifier
- Clinical summary
   - Active prescribed medications (generic nomenclature is required)
   - Historical prescribed medications and reason for discontinuation (generic nomenclature is required)
   - Other current non-prescribed (over the counter) medications
   - Allergy information
   - Diagnoses/problem list
   - Immunization status
- Results/reports
- Histories
   - Immunization history
   - Past medical history

- ❏ Surgical history
- ❏ Family history
- ❏ Social history
- Contact and registration information
    - ❏ Current address information and guarantor information
    - ❏ Healthcare durable power of attorney and proxy designees
        - ▪ Provide stored copy of durable power of attorney
    - ❏ Emergency contact(s)
    - ❏ Primary care physician
    - ❏ Other providers of care
- Current and historical insurance information

eHealth Tools

HIMSS encourages the development of ePHRs that provide an array of patient health tools that empower patients to make better personal healthcare decisions, comply with their healthcare regimen, improve the quality of their outcomes, and improve the efficiency of healthcare services. Specifically, these tools help patients maintain health and wellness, as well as manage chronic diseases. The tools must:

- Be simple to use through the application of appropriate human factors standards in user interface design;
- Be in non-clinician terms and be appropriate for an eighth grade reading level; and
- Employ both a "pull" and "push" content model where a patient can pull content from reliable resources and also allow the patient's providers to push information to the applications.

Examples of patient health tools include:
- ePHR usage and training materials
- Health maintenance
- Wellness and disease management
- Device data entry and display
- Provide current medical trial information based on diagnosis
- Diagnosis-based educational materials
- Services
    - ❏ Appointment scheduling
    - ❏ Prescription renewal

- eRefills (ability to communicate with a pharmacy to have refills delivered along with the ability to share this information with the original prescribing provider)
- eVisits
  - ❑ Information therapy
  - ❑ Education
  - ❑ Physician remote online care
- Interactive messaging
- Messaging transparency of healthcare institution and provider reports related to
  - ❑ Quality
  - ❑ Cost
  - ❑ Statistics

Technical

HIMSS champions the development of ePHRs providing technical assistance such as online help that must be available to assist constituents in the use and navigation of the ePHR, as well as addressing security issues and recommendations such as automatic logoffs, cache clearing, firewalls, anti-virus software, password standards, etc.

In addition, HIMSS encourages the development of ePHRs that provide technical support by telephone; ideally, this support would be available 24 hours a day, seven days a week.

Legal

As with EHRs, HIMSS acknowledges that there are a myriad of legal barriers to widespread ePHR adoption. HIMSS recommends development of national standards to ease burdens placed on constituents due to variances in state law and/or the development of national and uniform state rules, regulations and/or standards to address legal concerns raised by ePHRs such as ownership, access, control, reimbursement, rights and duties of constituents, limitations and liabilities raised by data quality, and privacy and security.

HIMSS supports ePHRs that have the ability to incorporate patient-entered data into their provider's legal medical record if the provider so chooses.

HIMSS acknowledges if a provider loads data from an EHR/EMR into a patient's ePHR, or if a patient uploads data from an ePHR into a provider EHR/EMR ePHR, legal issues are raised including, but not limited to:

- Patient responsibility for accurate and complete data entry and transfer
- Provider responsibility for reviewing patient entered data
- Reimbursement for provider-patient interaction through the ePHR
- Insurer responsibility
  - ❑ Reimbursement
  - ❑ Access
  - ❑ Transfer
  - ❑ Accuracy of data
- Rules and regulations
  - ❑ Reimbursement
  - ❑ Liability issues
  - ❑ Ownership issues
- Patient rights such as access, accounting, and amendment
- Liability for eHealth services and disclaimers regarding the limitations, rights, and responsibilities of patient and provider for e-health services
- Evolving definitions of legal medical records
- Variance between state laws
  - ❑ Directives
  - ❑ Authorized representative
  - ❑ Telemedicine
  - ❑ Unauthorized practice of medicine
- Interstate e-health services

HIMSS also supports ePHRs containing useful legal patient documents such as:
- Authorizations, advance health directives, consent forms and powers of attorney that specify who has access to the patient's PHI;
- Contact information such as for next of kin, legal counsel, guardian or *Ad Litem*; and
- Insurance information.

Medical Liability

Medical liability issues include, but are not limited to, the following:
- Holding a physician liable for more than the ordinary standard of care based on a "reasonable review" of a standard formal PHR;
- Holding a physician liable for providing care based on incomplete or inaccurate information contained in a PHR;
- Holding a physician liable for the act of consulting with a patient who lives in a state other than that in which the physician is licensed.

HIMSS supports that no additional barriers to clinician adoption of PHRs be created in addressing these liability issues such as requiring additional eHealth liability coverage or licensure, or as otherwise addressed in this document.

Financial

HIMSS supports the adoption of incentives by all constituents, including patients, payors, healthcare providers, healthcare institutions, pharmaceutical companies, device manufacturers and the federal and state governments of the United States to reduce the financial barriers to widespread ePHR adoption.

A barrier to ePHR adoption is the identification of a constituent who will fund the substantial costs of ePHR development, implementation, support, and maintenance. To date, the appropriate funding source to enable the widespread adoption of ePHRs in the United States has not emerged. ePHRs "tethered" to an institutional EHR/EMR are often offered as a market differentiator for provider institutions to attract new patients and create stronger liaisons with their patients. Such models are financed by the provider institution. This model, however, would serve as a disincentive to interoperable stand alone ePHRs that incorporate the pertinent individual's lifetime health information and encourage individuals to seek care at institutions with the best outcomes. Members of the constituent groups who presently provide ePHRs include all participants in the U.S. healthcare system: providers, payors, vendors, pharmaceutical companies, device manufacturers, the state and federal governments of the United States, etc. Studies of ePHR benefits of the various ePHR models will help to determine appropriate future ePHR funding.

Physician adoption of ePHRs is enhanced through the ability to do e-visit billing for ePHR "encounters," and through the creation of time-saving clinician practice efficiencies through ePHR workflow interaction. Further research is required to explore if ePHRs can truly increase clinician productivity, create revenue opportunities, and avoid unnecessary patient visits.

Summary

HIMSS supports the design and development of ePHRs as a tool that empowers healthcare consumers to manage and improve their health, positively influence behavioral decisions affecting health, enhance communication and a sense of partnership with health consumers and their health providers, and ultimately lower healthcare costs across our nation.

The HIMSS Personal Health Record Steering Committee wishes to acknowledge the following documents used as research sources in the creation of the HIMSS PHR Definition and Position Statement:

Friedman R (facilitator), Ratliff R (discussant). Personal health records—Registration and medication history. Presented at: Nationwide Health Information Network Forum, Office of the National Coordinator for Health Information Technology, U.S. Department of Health and Human Services; June 29, 2006; Washington, DC. Accessed online November 8, 2006.

Detmer D, Steen E. Learning from Abroad: Lessons and Questions on Personal Health Records for National Policy. AARP Public Policy Institute 2006; March 10, 2006. Accessed online November 8, 2006.

Cronin C. Personal Health Records: An Overview of What Is Available to the Public. AARP Public Policy Institute 2006; April 11, 2006. Accessed online November 8, 2006.

Personal Health Record Belongs to the Patient. AHIMA *Releases Definition, Attributes, and Data Elements of a Personal Health Record.* July 25, 2005. Accessed online November 8, 2006.

Innovations in Health Information Technology. America's Health Insurance Plan Center for Policy and Research. November 5, 2005. Accessed online November 8, 2006.

Ball MJ, Gold J. Banking on Health: Personal Records and Information Exchange. *Journal of Healthcare Information Management.* 2006; 20(2):71-83.

California HealthCare Foundation. California Can Lead the Way in Healthcare Information Technology: Recommendations to Governor Schwarzenegger's eHealth Action Forum. October, 2006. Accessed online November 8, 2006.

Office of the National Coordinator for Health Information Technology. Consumer Empowerment Background and Options Paper Breakthrough Models. February 21, 2006. Accessed online November 8, 2006.

Markle Foundation. Connecting for Health. Working Group on Policies for Electronic Information Sharing between Doctors and Patients. Connecting Americans to Their Healthcare. Executive Summary. July, 2004. Accessed online November 8, 2006.

Angst CM, Agarwal R, Downing J. An Empirical Examination of the Importance of Defining the PHR for Research and for Practice. Center for Health Information and Decision Systems, Department of Decision and Information Technologies; University of Maryland; College Park, MD. May 1, 2006. Accessed online November 8, 2006.

Collaborative Comments from the Consumer/Patient Working Group. Provided to the American Health Information Community (AHIC). Consumer/Patient Principles of Eight AHIC Breakthrough Initiatives. November 29, 2005. Accessed online November 8, 2006.

Clarke JL, Meiris DC. Electronic Personal Health Records Come of Age. (transcribed and adapted for publication.) *American Journal of Medical Quality.* Supplement to Vol. 21, No. 3, May/June, 2006. Accessed online November 8, 2006.

Conn J. Feds could have bigger role in PHR push; Health literacy a concern. *Modern Healthcare HITS: Beyond the Headlines.* September 19, 2006. Accessed online November 7, 2006.

Medem and the eRisk Working Group. eRisk for Providers: Understanding and Mitigating Provider Risk Associated with Online Patient Interaction. March, 2001. Accessed online November 8, 2006.

Fox LA, Sheridan PT. Personal Health Records: What's New? *Advance for Health Information Professionals.*16(13):10. June 16, 2006. Accessed online October 8, 2006.

Powner DA. Testimony before the Subcommittee on Federal Workforce and Agency Organization, Committee on Government Reform, House of Representatives.

Health Information Technology. HHS Is Continuing Efforts to Define Its National Strategy. September 1, 2006. Accessed online November 8, 2006.

Garets D, Davis M. Electronic Medical Records vs. Electronic Health Records: Yes, There Is a Difference. A HIMSS Analytics™ White Paper. Updated January 26, 2006. Accessed online November 8, 2006.

Moen A, Flatley Brennan P. Health@Home: The Work of Health Information Management in the Household (HIMH): Implications for Consumer Health. *Journal of the American Medical Informatics Association.* 2005;12:648–656.

Tang PC, Lansky D. The Missing Link: Bridging the Patient–Provider Health Information Gap. *Health Affairs Journal.* 2005(5) Sep: 24:1290-1295.

Burde HA. (presenter). Personal Health Records – It's Time…Legal Issues for PHRs. Presented at HIMSS Summer Summit, 2005. Accessed online November 8, 2006.

Motorola, Inc. IEEE-SA Health IT Standards Study Group. SIDEBAR: A Vision of Personalized Health Informatics Public. Version 1.13; 2006. Accessed online November 8, 2006.

Endsley S, Kibbe D, Linares A, Colorafi K. An Introduction to Personal Health Records. 2006. Family Practice Management Website of the American Academy of Family Physicians. Accessed online November 8, 2006.

Tang P, Ash JS, Bates DW, Overhage JM, Sands JZ. Personal Health Records: Definition, Benefits, and Strategies for Overcoming Barriers to Adoption. *Journal of the American Medical Informatics Association.* 2006;13(2):121-126. Accessed online November 8, 2006].

Markle Foundation. A Public-Private Collaboration. The Personal Health Working Group Final Report. July 1, 2003. Accessed online July 12, 2006.

Personal Health Records and Personal Health Record Systems: A Report and Recommendations from the National Committee on Vital and Health Statistics.

Washington, DC: National Institutes of Health, National Center for Health Statistics, Centers for Disease Control and Prevention. February, 2006. Accessed online November 8, 2006.

Agarwal R, Angst CM. Technology-Enabled Transformations in U.S. Health Care: Early Findings on Personal Health Records and Individual Use. November 22, 2004. University of Maryland: Robert H. Smith School of Business. Accessed online November 8, 2006.

Robeznieks A. Law Professor Warns AHIC on Potential Legal Woes of Electronic Records. *Modern Healthcare HITS: Beyond the Headlines.* September 20, 2006. Accessed online November 8, 2006.

Tang PC. PHR Definitions and Expectations: A Patient's Perspective. 2006. Palo Alto Medical Foundation. Sutter Health. Accessed online November 8, 2006.

Written Testimony on Personal Health Records for the American Health Information Community Consumer Empowerment Workgroup. Statement of Dr. David McCallie, Vice President of Informatics and

Chief Scientist, Cerner Corporation. July 27, 2006. Accessed online November 8, 2006.

Rethinking Potential of Personal Health Records Is Goal of New Robert Wood Johnson Foundation Program. July 17, 2006. Accessed online July 31, 2006.

CHAPTER 4

Evolving Market Forces Driving the Need for ePHRs

The comparatively poor quality relative to the high cost of healthcare in the U.S. is the driver of change to our healthcare system. Change is happening: consider the fact that public and private payors are increasing physician reimbursement for improved quality or not reimbursing for iatrogenic conditions. For example, CMS proposed "additional steps to strengthen the tie between the quality of care provided to Medicare beneficiaries and payment for the services provided when they are in the hospital. CMS is proposing to expand the list of conditions which are reasonably preventable through proper care and for which Medicare will no longer pay at a higher rate if the patient acquires them during a hospital stay."[1]

Employers are beginning to provide financial bonuses for employees demonstrating healthy behaviors such as smoking cessation or weight loss as well as financial penalties for individuals with persistent unhealthy behaviors. As these market forces are changing and affecting all healthcare constituents, appropriate financial structures are being designed and tested to support wellness and preventive medicine, improve healthcare quality and decrease costs.

The PHR is an ideal tool to facilitate this transformation. This chapter addresses the evolving market forces that will affect the doctor-patient relationship as well as the role the PHR can play to support healthcare constituents in developing partnerships.

THE EVOLVING DOCTOR-PATIENT RELATIONSHIP

The traditional physician-patient relationship is changing. Healthcare consumers are seeking to become better informed consumers. They are looking up medical information on the Internet in ever increasing numbers and want electronic access to their health records. Consumers want to become more empowered with regard to their healthcare. A combination of factors has contributed to the alteration in consumer demand:

- Negative reports: The highly publicized outcome reports such as IOM's *To Err is Human,* together with celebrated malpractice cases, highlight the fallibility of clinicians and hospitals and indicate that many patients die every year due to their doctors' mistakes.[2]
- Access to information: The accessibility of layperson-friendly medical information available on the Internet has helped consumers to become more educated about their healthcare conditions.
- Deterioration of relationship: The deterioration of the traditional doctor-patient relationship due to curtailing patient-focused services and limiting the visit to 10 or 15 minutes has caused these relationships to unravel.

Data supports that consumers should be more actively involved in their healthcare decisions, particularly regarding choice of providers and healthcare organizations. Despite the prevalence of this data, a 2002 Harris Interactive poll found that, "published lists of ratings [of hospitals, health plans and physicians], which rank different plans and providers, have had virtually no impact on consumer choice."[3]

There is a movement to make provider quality, outcome and cost data more readily available to consumers. A search of the Internet today regarding healthcare quality would yield multiple Web sites dedicated to this subject. Information regarding the importance of choosing providers and healthcare organizations as well as the tools to inform consumers should be readily available in ePHRs. The availability of this information might influence consumer healthcare decisions.

When an individual requires tertiary care, generally the patient will select a tertiary care provider covered by their insurance, recommended by their doctor, with an agreeable bedside manner or nearest to their home. Yet, when patients must undergo tertiary care, it is in their best interest to actively be engaged in the care decision-making process. This could be facilitated by having quality information available to consumers through ePHRs.

A patient generally will achieve better outcomes by finding the surgeon or care center that treats the most patients with the same disease. Such a care center is called a "center of excellence" and many studies have demonstrated that these centers and their clinicians achieve better outcomes at reduced costs. (This expression is used as a "term of art" rather than in the Medicare context.). One such study analyzed, "…the mortality associated with six different types of cardiovascular procedures and eight types of major cancer resections between 1994 and 1999 (total number of procedures, 2.5 million)… [They found] mortality decreased as volume increased for all 14 types of procedures, but the relative importance of volume varied markedly according to the type of procedure. [They concluded] In the absence of other information about the quality of surgery at the hospitals near them, Medicare patients undergoing selected cardiovascular or cancer procedures can significantly reduce their risk of operative death by selecting a high-volume hospital."[4] In fact, the volume/outcomes relationship is the cornerstone of state licensing and certificate of need programs for certain types of treatment and facilities in a variety of states.

Logically, this makes perfect sense. A surgeon and clinical team that perform hundreds or thousands of a particular kind of surgery every year are going to have a wealth of experience and knowledge regarding the disease entity—how best to evaluate a patient presenting with this problem; how best to manage the perioperative care, equip and staff the operating room for the surgery; how best to manage all of the phases of recovery and follow up. This is particularly evident if compared to a surgeon and clinical team that may see a few such cases per year, or worse yet, only one case every few years.

The following scenario illustrates the point: a surgeon is to perform surgery for a condition that he or she treats only very sporadically. The surgeon may realize the need to review the procedure in a textbook or through a literature search the night before the case. If the surgeon only reviews the textbook and does not do a full pertinent literature search, the technique described might not be up to date incorporating the latest research and best techniques. The scrub nurse is unfamiliar with the instruments required for the case and in what order the surgeon will need them. The surgical OR team is equally unfamiliar with the particular needs of the case. Additional instruments or other equipment may be required and will need to be located during the case, delaying the "skin-to-skin" time of the surgery.

Clearly, not doing this sort of surgery regularly means that the surgeon will take longer, prolonging the surgery and the patient's anesthesia exposure. To move this example further, the same may well be true of the initial evaluation, the postoperative recovery, hospitalization and follow up care; all contributing to increased costs as well as the likelihood of poorer outcomes. In a complex case, the surgeon may not be aware of factors that may directly influence outcomes such as tests that are required to appropriately determine the precise surgical procedure to be performed, as well as the correct staging of a patient that could influence postoperative treatments or increase the possibility of the need for future additional surgery.

The example above is used to illustrate the importance of having information regarding provider and healthcare center quality, outcomes and cost information readily available to healthcare consumers in PHRs. To empower patients to make the best decisions regarding their health, PHR tools should include educational information about the importance of researching your provider; asking your provider questions; and how to choose a center of excellence for care as well as supplying provider and healthcare organization report cards.

Transparent information about providers and healthcare organizations needs to be available in ePHRs. Such information should include the number of cases annually at the organization, outcomes, quality reports and costs. For healthcare organizations, however, the cost information may be difficult to provide because the organization may have different negotiated costs with different payors.

Enhanced consumer empowerment and awareness regarding healthcare will directly affect costs and quality of U.S. healthcare and is an essential element to changing our medical model. Recipients of tertiary care should be able to review comparative data regarding tertiary care centers, select the center for their care based on the centers outcomes and costs, and have their insurance cover their choice.

In many communities, there are not enough patients that need the service provided to support the number of cases for a medical center to be a center of excellence. Publication of care outcomes and costs will allow healthcare consumers the ability to make informed healthcare decisions. If there are multiple centers in the community providing the same service without an adequate case population to allow each to be a center of excellence, appropriate informed consumer choice may drive out provider redundancy of service. This action could drive down healthcare costs while improving quality and outcomes in the community. The PHR will be a tool for not only informing consumers about their conditions, but a vehicle for informing them about care choices as well.

A fundamental aspect of this change is consumer empowerment through knowledge—knowledge that could come from tools and information provided through ePHRs. Consumer empowerment will lead to a shift in the patient–physician relationship, and it is not surprising that this shift might be threatening to healthcare providers. But there are other reasons: physicians are feeling additional market forces affecting their bottom line beyond consumer choice and empowerment.

SHIFTING MARKET FORCES FOR PHYSICIANS

Pay for performance (P4P) is the basis for the new healthcare reimbursement model proposed by CMS. As CMS stated in a press release announcing the model, "Medicare has various initiatives to encourage improved quality of care in all health care settings where Medicare beneficiaries receive their health care services, including physicians' offices and ambulatory care facilities, hospitals, nursing homes, home health care agencies and dialysis facilities.

The foundation of effective pay-for-performance initiatives is collaboration with providers and other stakeholders, to ensure that valid quality measures are used, that providers aren't being pulled in conflicting directions, and that providers have support for achieving actual improvement...Through these collaborative efforts, CMS is developing and implementing a set of pay-for-performance initiatives to support quality improvement in the care of Medicare beneficiaries."[5]

Essentially, under this model, physicians would be reimbursed for practicing nationally agreed upon evidence-based best medicine. The aim of such a model is to have physicians be reimbursed for superior patient outcomes. The ultimate goal of a P4P model is to improve healthcare quality and outcomes, while decreasing medical errors and costs. To realize the goals of attaining superior outcomes and refocus primary care on preventive medicine to decrease national healthcare costs, there are two constituent groups that must be engaged toward achieving the goals. Physicians must practice evidence-based medicine and healthcare consumers must bear the responsibility for complying with their medical regimens as well as their lifestyle and healthcare choices.

Recognizing the true bilateral constituent basis required to achieve these goals, it is clear that both of the constituent groups must be motivated. A new partnership needs to be formed where the healthcare consumer is an equally responsible partner and both partners are incented to achieve the same goals.

As the physician-consumer interaction evolves, consumers will expect and demand control of their own information via transportable, consumer-controlled ePHRs with links to transparent provider information regarding healthcare quality, outcomes, cost, convenience and services. With such control, there is associated responsibility: Individuals could withhold or delete their health information, making it inaccessible to providers. These actions might result in inappropriate or incorrect treatment that must not be attributed to the clinician.

Creating an effective incentive model will drive appropriate consumer healthcare behavior and function as a catalyst in the evolution of the physician-patient relationship.

PARADIGM SHIFT FOR THE CONSUMER: EXTERNAL DRIVERS TOWARD CONSUMER ADOPTION OF ePHRS

The growing trend of holding healthcare consumers accountable for their behaviors will influence consumer adoption of ePHRs.

- In October 2006, a story in the *British Medical Journal (BMJ) News* indicated that the German government was planning to make cancer patients that did not undergo recommended cancer screening prior to their diagnoses pay more for their cancer treatments then the patients that had undergone regular screening.[6] Previously, the only publicized model of incentives for healthcare consumer behavior in the U.S. was one where smokers were required to pay more for their life insurance.

- Recently, there has been a trend towards employers and insurers wielding both incentives and disincentives to encourage consumers to adopt healthy behaviors. Many employers have completely banned smoking from any part of the grounds of their facilities; a large Ohio IDN announced that they will not hire new personnel who smoke. More recently, employers have begun to tie financial consequences to their employee behaviors.

- IBM pays $150 to employees whose children complete a 12-week online program for diet and exercise training. In addition, the company has an employee wellness program that includes financial incentives for employees for their participation in a variety of programs including: smoking cessation, weight loss, using a pre-populated ePHR, taking health assessments, disease management and exercise. IBM reports an investment of $20 million has resulted in a $100 million per year savings for the company in healthcare costs alone. This data did not include consideration of the financial impact of work absenteeism.

- Pitney Bowes offers their employees free clinics, fitness programs and low cost/free medications. The results of their programs have been a single digit increase in their healthcare costs relative to a comparable double digit increase in the market.[7]

Other employers have begun charging additional healthcare insurance fees to their employees with obesity, uncontrolled hypertension or uncontrolled elevated cholesterol. Clearly, we have reached an era in which economic forces are driving the trend toward increased consumers' accountability for health-related behaviors that will ultimately affect their health and their disease-related morbidity and mortality. In such an environment, consumers will be motivated to comply with preventive medicine and chronic disease management regimens as well as to consistently practice more healthy behaviors.

EPHR AS THE OPTIMAL TOOL TO SUPPORT HEALTHCARE CONSUMER BEHAVIORAL CHANGE

Behavioral change theory purports that people are ready to act (in this case, make healthy behavior changes) if they believe they are susceptible to the condition (perceived susceptibility); believe the condition has serious consequences (perceived severity); believe taking action will reduce their susceptibility to the condition or its severity (perceived benefits); believe the costs of taking action (perceived barriers) are outweighed by the benefits; are exposed to factors that prompt action (cues to action); and are confident in their ability to successfully perform an action (self-efficacy).

Behavioral change theory further identifies successful strategies to assist the individual to change and maintain the change as follows:

- **Perceived susceptibility**: define level of risk of a population, tailor information based on characteristics or behaviors, help an individual develop an accurate perception of his or her own risk
- **Perceived benefits**: explain how, where and when to take action and what the potential positive results will be
- **Perceived severity**: specify the consequences of a condition and recommend action
- **Perceived barriers**: offer reassurance, incentives and assistance; correct misinformation
- **Cues to action**: provide the "how to" information, promote awareness, employ reminder systems
- **Self-efficacy**: instill confidence in one's ability to take action; verbal persuasion; role modeling (peer modeling and demonstration of desired behaviors); use of progressive goal setting, verbal reinforcement.[8]

A well designed ePHR would include tools that support the strategies to assist the individual to change health behaviors and maintain the change. Individuals may allow their data—including behavioral, clinical, pharmacy, billing, demographic, genetic, healthcare spending and outcomes—to be used for extensive predictive modeling studies. The information garnered from such studies could actively be reflected back to healthcare consumers through the ePHR. Consumers could be made aware that changing one or more behaviors has the potential to affect their longevity and quality of life as well as financial implications as reflected through a health/wealth equation.

Ideally, tools in the ePHR would directly address all of the defined strategies for behavioral change. We can imagine a graphical representation with morbidity and mortality as one axis and time as the other. One line would represent the ideal outcomes with optimal behaviors and the other would represent the predicted outcome with actual behaviors. ePHR tools would prompt consumers to adopt healthy behaviors leading to a narrowing of the difference between the actual and predicted lines. Such a tool would encompass most of the behavioral change theory strategies thereby aiding the individual in achieving the best possible personal health outcomes.

PHR BEHAVIORAL CHANGE TOOLS
Predictive Modeling

As previously discussed in Chapter 3, large population studies could decrease healthcare costs through a new best practice care model: personalized medicine. Two large epidemiological studies that were begun in the 20th century—the Framingham Heart Study and the Nurses' Health Study—have yielded remarkable advances in identifying preventable risk factors related to heart disease, stroke, cancer and many other maladies. A major element of the significance of these studies was the pairing of behavioral data with clinical data. The analysis of this data facilitated what is now common knowledge regarding everything from the relationship of cholesterol, diet and exercise to heart disease, to the combined estrogen and testosterone hormone replacement therapy being correlated with an increased risk of breast cancer,[9] to the observation that eating an ounce of nuts five times per week is related to a reduced risk of developing type 2 diabetes.[10] The Framingham study alone has yielded over

1,000 scientific papers and the analysis of the data from both studies continues to result in significant information, particularly regarding behavioral or controllable risk factors of disease.

The ideal future PHR or EHR models would be one where—using a standardized data paradigm—clinical data from all sources, self-reported behavioral data, genetic data, and home and implanted medical device data could be collated. If millions of individuals agreed to allow their de-identified data to be used for epidemiological studies, analysis of this rich data pool could transform our understanding of the genesis and progression of disease. Predictive models using the data would facilitate an understanding of the genetic, environmental and behavioral elements contributing to a given individual's health or disease processes. This comprehension could permanently alter healthcare to a personalized model of care delivery.

Data from such studies could segment populations of patients and identify what patients would best respond to what treatments, leading physicians to practice directed personalized medicine. For example, instead of prescribing an initial medication that is either ineffective or not tolerated by a specific patient and then trying a second and possible third medication until finding a successful treatment, a clinician could make an informed selection based on the patient's precise profile as to which of the myriad of medications available for a specific condition would be correct for that patient. The precise medicine selected based on the patient's profile would have, for that patient, the highest efficacy and the lowest side effects. Personalized medicine would decrease healthcare costs. From the above example, the expense from the first two medications that were prescribed and not tolerated by the patient would be eliminated.

Results of predictive modeling would also allow targeted ePHR "sentinel" tools to be developed to alert and remind individuals regarding specific, personalized behavioral and preventive medicine and care management regimens. An example of a tool that could inspire an individual to change their behaviors and enable them to track their behavioral change progress relative to their predicted long term health is illustrated in Figure 4-1. The top line represents their personal predicted declining health over time if the individual persists in their current poor behavioral habits, such as lack of exercise, smoking, and a fast food diet. The second and third lines represent the individuals predicted health outcome progress after she has improved her health related behavior over six months, and two years, respectively. The fourth line represents the individuals' predicted health outcomes assuming long-term compliance with a healthy behavioral regimen.

Figure 4-1. Proposed Personalized Predictive Behavior – Health Outcomes PHR Tool

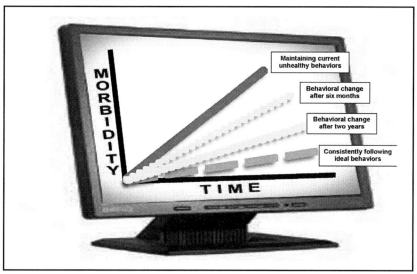

Well designed ePHRs would include tools and alerts:
• To empower healthcare consumers with knowledge to enhance their health-related decision making;
• To aid in the communication between health constituents;
• To allow for consumer directed flow of their health information;
• To help adherence to health regimens and health maintenance; and
• To link consumer constituents in supportive communities to achieve "contagious health" networks.

SOCIAL NETWORK

Anyone who has ever tried to lose weight, stop smoking, comply with a medication regimen or modify their behavior in some way knows that this can be extremely difficult.

A 2007 *New England Journal of Medicine* article based on the Framingham population found that obesity is actually contagious. The article states that, "...[a] person's chances of becoming obese increased by 57 percent (95 percent confidence interval [CI], 6 to 123) if he or she had a friend who became obese ...[and]...obesity appears to spread through social ties."[11]

It appears that behaviors resulting in unwanted outcomes can be spread through social networks. We already know that PHRs can be designed to promote healthy behaviors in the individual, but can we design PHRs that can be used to promote health and wellness transformation in a community through "contagious health"? Can we design PHRs from which individuals can release their data to participate in national population studies leading to predictive modeling that ultimately will transform the practice of medicine to a personalized medical model?

In addition to the behavioral change strategies noted above, the prevailing thought regarding the promotion and maintenance of behavioral change is that such change occurs in a system (i.e., a personal system, a family system, a community system) and is associated with the use of a specific set of strategies to change a behavioral system to achieve a specific goal. PHRs that utilize strategies for system change implemented throughout a healthcare consumer community might influence a "contagious health" or positive change throughout the community.

A system behavioral change approach focuses less on individual motivation than on building habitual healthy behaviors into day-to-day routines. It includes the involvement of the social environment surrounding the people interested in making behavioral changes in order to effectively promote success in the face of wavering individual motivation. In addition to the above tools being available for the individual, the consumer could open up the behavioral change support tools to access a social network of like individuals as well as to rely on their personal support network. In so doing, existing and enhanced coaching ePHR tools could be designed to support a community or system focused on making and maintaining positive health-related behavioral change.

PHYSICIAN AND HEALTHCARE CONSUMER ACCOUNTABILITY: SHIFTING INCENTIVES TO TRANSFORM AND FORGE A NEW PHYSICIAN-PATIENT PARTNERSHIP

To transform medicine in the U.S., we must increase the focus of healthcare on preventive medicine, chronic disease management, improve healthcare quality and outcomes, and decrease healthcare costs.

To achieve these goals, it is essential that all healthcare constituents be motivated. The following steps would help achieve these goals:

- Financial motivation for all healthcare constituents (payors, employers, pharmacies, providers, consumers, etc.) causing alignment toward the goals.
- Providing enabling HIT tools, such as standards based interoperable EHRs with integration of all healthcare constituents' data and workflows, with the ultimate control of the data given to consumers to support a patient-centered care model.
- Having ePHRs that encompass all required consumer healthcare tools but also having tools to enable community-based "contagious health."
- Creating a financially sustainable business model to support the required HIT tools.
- Requiring the measurement and reporting of real morbidity and mortality outcomes rather than surrogate measures for these outcomes.
- Mandating outcomes reporting and making this information publicly available to consumers through the ePHR.
- Creating incentives to motivate individuals to achieve their best possible outcomes regarding their health.

Holding all healthcare constituents financially accountable for quality outcomes will more rapidly enhance the adoption of the necessary steps by all of the involved healthcare groups toward achieving these goals.

Only through the financial motivation of healthcare constituents can we reach the shared goals of improving healthcare quality, outcomes and decreasing costs. PHRs will be one of the enabling HIT technologies toward these outcomes and will help to redefine the physician–patient relationship as a partnership.

REFERENCES

1. Centers for Medicare and Medicaid Services. CMS proposes to expand quality program for hospital inpatient services in FY 2009 [press release]. April 14, 2008. Available at: http://www.cms.hhs.gov/apps/media/press/release.asp?Counter=30 41&intNumPerPage=10&checkDate=&checkKey=&srchType=1&numDays=350 0&srchOpt=0&srchData=&srchOpt=0&srchData=&keywordType=All&chkNew sType=1%2C+2%2C+3%2C+4%2C+5&intPage=&showAll=&pYear=&year=&d esc=&cboOrder=date. Accessed June 12, 2008.

2. Institute of Medicine. *To Err is Human: Building a Safer Health Care System.* Washington, DC: National Academy Press; 1999.

3. Taylor H, Leitman R, ed. Quality ratings have almost no influence on consumers' choices of hospitals, health plans and physicians. *Harris Interactive Health Care News.* October 11, 2002. Available at: http://www.harrisinteractive.com/news/ newsletters/healthnews/HI_HealthCareNews2002Vol2_Iss19.pdf. Accessed June 12, 2008.

4. Birkmeyer JD, Siewers AE, Finlayson EVA, et al. Hospital volume and surgical mortality in the United States. *N Engl J Med.* 2002; 346:1128-1137.

5. Centers for Medicare and Medicaid Services. Medicare "pay for performance" initiatives [press release]. January 31, 2005. Available at: http://www.cms.hhs. gov/apps/media/press/release.asp?Counter=1343. Accessed June 12, 2008.

6. BMJ 28th October, 2006.

7. Promoting the Use of Healthcare IT. Presentation to the Public Programs Implementation Taskforce of the State Alliance for e-Health of the National Governors Association. April 22, 2008.

8. Bandura A. *Social Foundations of Thought and Action.* Englewood Cliffs, New Jersey: Prentice-Hall; 1986.

9. Tamimi, R., Endogenous hormone levels, mammographic density, and subsequent risk of breast cancer in postmenopausal women. *Archives of Internal Medicine.* 2006; 166(14):1483-1489.

10. Rui Jiang, et al. Nut and peanut butter consumption and risk of type 2 diabetes in women. *JAMA.* 2002; 288:2554-2560.

11. Christakis NA, Fowler JH. The spread of obesity in a large social network over 32 years. *NEJM.* July 26, 2007; 357(4):370-379.

CHAPTER 5

Physicians, Patients and PHRs

The previous chapter addressed the evolving market forces that will both drive the evolution of PHRs and compel healthcare constituents to use them. This chapter is an analysis of the current state of, and barriers to, PHR adoption among clinicians and healthcare consumers.

PHYSICIAN INTERACTION WITH PHRS

There are at least three components to the interaction between physicians and PHRs: (1) willingness to use data from PHRs; (2) willingness to push data to PHRs; and (3) the use of PHRs as a vehicle for communication to promote health and wellness. Although PHRs have frequently been touted as tools for healthcare consumer empowerment, to date these tools have not been widely embraced or adopted by clinicians. What have been the clinician barriers to adoption of PHRs?

CHANGE IN THE PHYSICIAN–PATIENT RELATIONSHIP PARADIGM

The PHR supports a paradigm shift toward an empowered healthcare consumer and away from a traditional paternalistic medical practice model. Some physicians continue to feel that consumers are not equipped to understand their medical information in the absence of physician intermediation. This group is concerned that any abnormal information will cause their patients anxiety and, therefore, consumers should only have access to their information as interpreted by the clinician. They may want to maintain their position as the ultimate arbiter of their patient's healthcare and knowledge about their conditions. Yet patients' access to visits with their clinicians is becoming more difficult. The time of an ambulatory visit has been abbreviated and hospital stays have been dramatically shortened. The result is that patients seen in ambulatory settings today are significantly sicker than in the past. There is a growing need for consumers to self-manage their chronic diseases, comply with treatment plans and recommended behaviors and complete all of the primary and secondary disease prevention tests and vaccinations recommended.

For years individuals seeking medical information have been searching the Internet. For many physicians, an empowered healthcare consumer has upset the status quo. Some clinicians do not want to participate in PHR programs that they experience as challenging their role. Consumer demand for PHR participation by their physicians may positively affect this reluctance on the part of clinicians to use PHRs. These are significant concerns on the part of the clinicians. The PHR represents a fundamental paradigm shift in their medical practice model toward partnering with patients in their care.

MORE WORK WITHOUT ADDITIONAL REIMBURSEMENT FOR ALREADY OVERBURDENED CLINICIANS

In general, physicians are apprehensive that PHRs will represent more work for them and that this work will not be reimbursed and may create additional liabilities. In the absence of interfaced and integrated systems enabling the flow of discrete information through an EMR,

EHR, and PHR, the physician would be obliged to engage in time-consuming behaviors of accessing the patient's PHR over the Internet and manually downloading information to or from a patient's PHR. Clinicians are concerned that the interpretation of outside results will fall to them, and that their patients will request them to interpret minor result abnormalities and inundate them with questions sent through a PHR. A 2008 paper on the experiences of three organizations that have implemented PHRs found that the volume of secure health messages to clinicians through the PHR remained stable over time. For example, one of the organizations, Beth Israel Deaconess Medical Center, reported that, "...we found the number of messages handled by physicians is quite modest, on the order of 20 messages per month per 100 patients, replacing a roughly equal number of phone calls."[1] A 2005 study of secure Web messaging through a tethered PHR from the University of California Davis Health System found that, "Patients were overwhelmingly satisfied, and providers and staff were generally satisfied: both found the system easy to use." In addition, "Physicians' fears of being overwhelmed by electronic patient messages proved groundless."[2]

NEW LIABILITIES

Physicians are concerned about introducing new liabilities through the PHR. They may have access to information supplied by the patient that they never had before, either information pertaining to patient data entry between visits or information from outside sources. This issue is addressed more thoroughly in Chapter 8.

OVERCOMING CLINICIAN ADOPTION BARRIERS

Electronic Data Flow That Supports the Clinical Practice Model

Physician acceptance of PHRs may depend upon the ease of transmission and receipt of data. Provider adoption will likely be correlated with the extent that patient information automatically flows between the provider's EMR and the individual's PHR and vice-versa. For information coming from an outside source to the clinician through the PHR, only true data integration into the clinician's EMR supports their workflow. It is difficult to imagine that a physician would be pleased about taking time from a 10- to 15-minute visit to log out of their EMR and log into an Internet-based PHR to review data that can only be incorporated into their own electronic system manually. Data exchange that is automated or "pushed" to the end user is preferred over data that must be "pulled" from another system. Physicians would want PHR data to be date, time, and source-stamped and pushed to the correct field of their EMR. For example, if the patient releases the PHR problem list to a new physician practicing with an EMR, the physician would want these diagnoses to be incorporated into the problem list field of their EMR, date time and source stamped, and flagged for review. With this level of integration, the physician could readily review with the patient and edit any new information coming across from the PHR to his or her EMR at the time of the visit. Clinicians who are not yet using an EMR would either need to print or manually transcribe information from the patient's PHR into their paper record.

There is not an abundance of information regarding the clinician benefits of their patients using a PHR. Most of the available data comes from health systems using EMR tethered PHRs and largely supports actual efficiency gains for providers. An unpublished time-motion study of physicians and their support staff working in an ambulatory setting using a tethered PHR with secure physician-patient messaging and result release found significant time savings for both the providers and their support staff with regard to communicating results to patients through the PHR relative to the traditional mailed result letter.[3]

Information regarding the nursing experience using Partners' PHR, called Patient Gateway, affirmed that, "Nurses find Gateway promotes greater efficiency and time management."[4]

A May 2008 survey found that the reasons provider organizations have launched PHRs are "…to encourage personal health management among their population, …improve treatment adherence and compliance, increase patient retention and satisfaction, stay competitive with other organizations offering PHRs, reduce healthcare and coverage costs, build brand awareness and loyalty and streamline processes."[5]

The same survey reported that of the 63 organizations that have implemented PHRs and responded to the survey, "…many are experiencing great success."[5]

Providers and patients alike appreciate the concept of a pre-visit questionnaire that can be completed online in the PHR. The questionnaire would be completed by the individual prior to the visit, pushed to and integrated into the clinician's EMR, then edited by the provider and included as part of the visit documentation into the EMR at the time of the visit.

To enable data entry by the patient in the PHR, the information must be mapped from medical terminology (such as an ICD or CPT code) to lay-person friendly terms that the patient will understand. Such mapping of medical terminology to lay-friendly terms also facilitates the data entry as discrete data which can flow from the PHR to the EMR and be available for reporting and research purposes. When this is accomplished, the PHR will be an effective communications and initial data entry vehicle that has the potential to decrease the clinician's workload and create additional care efficiency.

CATALYTIC REINFORCEMENT MODEL FOR AN EVOLVED PHYSICIAN–PATIENT PARTNERSHIP

Finally, part of physicians embracing PHRs may involve accepting the evolving model of the physician–patient relationship. Clearly, the most powerful method of motivating clinicians to accept this model will involve financial incentives and disincentives. A successful financial incentive model will reward both patients and physicians for focusing on preventive medicine and achieving actual improved outcomes.

THE CHANGING PROFILE OF HEALTHCARE CONSUMERS

The medical paradigm began to shift for healthcare consumers with the development of the Internet. For the first time, healthcare consumers could have up-to-date, layperson-friendly health information over the Web. According to reports regarding Internet searches, health information has always been one of the most popular.

Well-publicized healthcare quality reports and malpractice cases in the lay press regarding iatrogenic or physician-caused deaths and morbidities have also made consumers aware of the need to become empowered regarding their healthcare.

THE SILVER TSUNAMI

The baby boomers have had a significant influence on everything in the U.S., and they currently have a major influence on consumer demands and expectations surrounding healthcare—and will continue to do so in the future. In the U.S., one of the largest segments of the population continues to be the baby boomers, those individuals born between 1945 and 1965. The U.S. population of baby boomers that will be 65 or older by the year 2030 will increase to 71.5 million. The aging of this population has been called "the silver tsunami" and appears to be directly correlated to the rise in healthcare as a percentage of the GDP.

Delayed childbirth and increased longevity have spawned the phenomenon of the "sandwich generation," meaning those individuals who are responsible for caring for their children may simultaneously be responsible for caring for their elderly parent or parents. This generation is interested in PHRs, not only for coordinating their own care and promoting their own health and wellness, but also to aid in the coordination of the care of their loved ones.

Healthy Life Style

The Baby Boomers claim to be driven by a healthier lifestyle. Therefore, they would be interested in PHR tools that would support them in their efforts. In a 2006 survey, half of baby boomers surveyed want to live longer, two out of five want to look better, and one third want to reduce the effects of aging.[6] Another survey found that 71 percent want to maintain their health, 52 percent have started thinking about a healthier lifestyle, 75 percent feel that they have some control over preventing disease and 85 percent believe that through proper nutrition they can prevent disease.[7]

Cost Sensitivity and Comparison Shopping

Consumers are seeking to manage their healthcare spending, shopping for the best prices for their medications online. Some are seeking to purchase their medications in Canada where, "Estimates indicate that buying medicines from a certified Canadian pharmacy can save Americans 20%–80% on brand name drugs."[8]

Many predict that more Americans will be searching the Web for healthcare quality and pricing. As *Healthcare IT News* reports, "If Health and Human Services Secretary Michael Leavitt has it his way, one day before 2014, Americans will be able to search online for pricing information on healthcare the way they can search for plane tickets today on Web sites such as Travelocity."[9]

Several established healthcare practices have begun to post the fees for their services online to compete with businesses such as Take Care™ or Minute Clinic™—retail clinics that offer a new care delivery paradigm based on a convenience, quality and a low-cost delivery model.

Service

Customer service is traditionally an afterthought in the healthcare industry. A study funded by the Robert Wood Johnson (RWJ) Foundation in 2000 found that, "Access-to-care findings—including problems contacting the provider, getting an appointment and having an unmet need—were more unfavorable for HMO plans and were associated with lower levels of enrollee satisfaction. Many specific results on a wide range of measures of patient/physician interpersonal communication and quality of services were especially unfavorable to HMOs."[10]

The HCAHPS, or CAHPS Hospital Survey Chartbook, is a survey of patients hospitalized during 2006. For this publication, 927 U.S. hospitals voluntarily submitted their survey results representing a total of 190,690 respondents. The survey results were released in 2007. Of note, only 66.3 percent of respondents indicated that they were definitely willing to recommend the hospital where they were treated, 58 percent indicated that the hospital was always quiet and clean, and 56 percent indicated that hospital staff were always responsive. On the positive side, 77 percent of respondents indicated that the doctors always communicated with them and 69 percent indicated that nurses always communicated with them.[11]

Harris Interactive® polls tracked public perceptions of whether the healthcare industry is doing a good or bad job of serving their customer needs from 1997–2001. The public's perception regarding hospitals, pharmaceutical or drug companies, health insurance companies, and managed care companies, dropped every year. In 2001, the percent of those surveyed indicating that their customer needs were served was: 67 percent for hospitals; 59 percent for drug companies; 39 percent for health insurance companies; and 29 percent for managed care companies.[12]

Likely as a response to this dissatisfaction with health-related clinical services, there is a rise in clinicians offering special "concierge" medical services for which patients pay a premium to the doctor providing the service. Such concierge services may include a guarantee of same-day appointments with the doctor and house calls. PHRs certainly can be utilized to efficiently enhance provider access and services. Consumers can access a PHR over the Internet at any time.

Medical Tourism

There is a growing number of medical tourism opportunities allowing patients to elect to travel abroad for their medical care, paying out of pocket and knowing that these providers are not under U.S. licensure or jurisdiction. This trend may be driven in part by consumers seeking lower costs through having their procedures abroad, their desire for on-demand service and by the notion of a combined procedure/ vacation, lower costs, quality and the exotic. This may be particularly true for boomers who are obsessed with a youthful appearance and have the opportunity to undergo their plastic surgery at a lower cost in an exotic location where they are anonymous and are pampered during their recovery. PHRs and EHRs could support the continuum of care for patients' medical tourism activities through allowing the international exchange of health data, provided that there are international standards developed for health information exchange.

Consumer Empowerment

Consumer empowerment and the changing attitudes of consumers toward PHRs have previously been discussed. It is clear that consumers are becoming increasingly informed and interested in healthcare and treatments. A Harris Poll found that 84 percent of all online adult Americans search the Internet for health information and 76 percent of adults over the age of 55 use the Web to diagnose their medical conditions.[13]

Boomer Consumers and Technology

It is important not to discount the interest in technology of adults who did not grow up with these mediums: "Eight out of ten boomers surveyed report that they are comfortable using new technology, and that technology is a vital part of their lives; 95 percent report that they use email regularly, 81 percent report that they use technology to stay connected with their families, and 62 percent report that they purchase products over the Internet."[7]

Very limited data is available about which healthcare consumers are actually using the PHRs that are offered. One study of the users of a tethered PHR in a large IDN found that "The only predictors of degree of ePHR use among the Registered Users are, number of diagnoses from the EMR problem list and the number of clinical encounters… [This tethered] ePHR portal appears to be most useful to patients who are sicker and greater consumers of healthcare." The authors conclude that, "This indicates the need to offer more functionality to support and encourage healthy behavior and lifestyle choices for individuals before they develop specific illnesses."[14]

A Harris Interactive poll in 2004 found that, "two in five adults (42 percent) keep personal or family health records…[and] almost everyone (84 percent) of those who do not thought that it was a good idea to do so."[15] It also found that "…older people are more likely than younger people to keep personal or family medical records."[15]

Drivers for an Individual's Healthcare Decisions

Healthcare consumers continue to be most likely to listen to their doctors' recommendations regarding their healthcare decisions. However, in recent surveys of healthcare consumers, the Internet is now being cited as a source for healthcare decisions.

In addition, healthcare consumers are considering many factors related to their healthcare decisions including cost, service, convenience, ease of access (appointment availability, parking), kindness and politeness of staff, provider's bedside manner, tastefully decorated waiting rooms with magazines of interest, and timely and caring communications from the clinician.

Though all of the above factors will be part of a healthcare consumer's decision-making process, if consumers are educated about the differences in quality and outcomes among providers and healthcare centers, they may select to choose those centers that report the best quality. Relevant tools need to be provided in PHRs to enable consumers to compare providers and hospitals across the parameters of quality, cost, convenience, service and consumer satisfaction.

The factors influencing healthcare consumer decisions are rapidly evolving as is the receptivity healthcare consumers have to PHRs.

BARRIERS TO CONSUMER ADOPTION OF PHRS

Privacy and Security

Conventional barriers to consumer adoption of, or interest in PHRs have been related to concerns about privacy and security. Prior surveys demonstrated that 42 percent of Americans feel privacy risks outweigh the expected benefits of electronic health records. Seventy-seven percent of Americans fear that their data in electronic records will be used for purposes other than their healthcare, like marketing.[17]

With PHRs and PHR platforms now being offered by small companies and corporate giants such as Google and Microsoft, it is clear that such entities are not covered under HIPAA. To gain and maintain the public trust in these systems, some standards of privacy, security, and clarity of terms and conditions of use (particularly as they pertain to secondary uses of data) must be developed, and adherence monitored. "Consumers navigating the opportunities to share and potentially even monetize their data for research deserve a guidepost such as a certification or a seal of approval with regard to services, software, and projects from a trusted authority."[18]

Fortunately, CCHIT has recently launched a PHR certification development project that will focus in large part on PHR privacy and security. CCHIT certification, once awarded, can be prominently displayed on PHR sites that have been certified. The public can then be educated regarding the implications of certification, and made aware of how to recognize PHR products that meet the certification standards and those that do not. As many PHRs and PHR platforms are linked to a variety of additional Web sites, perhaps the consumer should be warned when they are leaving a CCHIT certified PHR.

In addition to CCHIT certification, the Markle Foundation has developed and published Connecting for Health Core Principles to "provide the foundation for managing personal health information within consumer-accessible data streams." The Markle Foundation work rises in importance because its guidelines have been voluntarily adopted by the following PHR or PHR platform providers to the consumer market: Dossia, Google, Intuit, Microsoft, and WebMD. The Markle Foundation Common Framework for PHRs includes several interrelated component guidelines under two headings, "Consumer Policy" and "Consumer Technology." The Consumer Policy guidelines include: (CP1) Overview; (CP2) Policy Notice to Consumers; (CP3) Consumer Consent to Collections, Uses, and Disclosures of Information; (CP4) Chain-of-Trust Agreements; (CP5) Notification of Misuse or Breach; (CP6) Dispute Resolution; (CP7) Discrimination and Compelled Disclosures; (CP8) Consumer Obtainment and Control of Information; and (CP9) Enforcement of Policies. The Technology Policies include: (CT1) Technology Overview; (CT2) Authentication of Consumers; (CT3) Immutable Audit Trails; (CT4) Limitations on Identifying Information; (CT5) Portability of Information; (CT6) Security and Systems Requirements; and (CT7) Architecture for Consumer Participation.[19]

Source of the PHR

Consumer surveys have demonstrated that it appears to make a significant difference to consumers which constituency group is offering the PHR. Fifty-nine percent of healthcare consumers do not trust their health insurer.[20] Fifty-three percent of Americans are very concerned about health insurers gaining access to their electronic health records. Therefore, it may be difficult for individuals to accept PHRs offered by their insurers. Individuals initially appear to be more interested in tethered PHRs offered by their healthcare providers due to their mistrust of their employers and their insurers. A Harris Poll found that "Health insurance providers ranked highest in public distrust. Fifty-nine percent of adult respondents say that their general trust for insurance companies is 'not much' or 'not at all' while 29 percent say that their own trust in their insurer is not much or not at all."[20]

It will be interesting to see how consumers respond to the commercial PHRs mentioned above prior to and after CCHIT certification is implemented.

Consumers Want Electronic Access to Their Health Information

More recent surveys have demonstrated that there is a dramatic shift in consumer attitudes about electronic and personal health records. A November, 2007 Wall Street Journal Online/Harris Interactive Health-Care Poll found that, "A sizable majority of Americans believe electronic medical records have the potential to improve U.S. health care and that the benefits outweigh privacy risks." And a vast majority of Americans want access to their health information: "Ninety-one percent of those polled say patients should have access to their own electronic records maintained by their physician."[21]

A Markle survey from 2006 indicated that an overwhelming majority of U.S. adults feels that access to their medical records for themselves and for their doctors is important. "Ninety-seven percent think it's important for their doctors to be able to access all of their medical records in order to provide the best care; 96 percent think it's important for individuals to be able to access all of their own medical records to manage their own health; two in three Americans (65 percent) would like to access all of their own medical information across an electronic network. This interest spans demographic groups—with a majority (53 percent) of Americans 60 and older and high proportions of minority groups expressing interest. When given the scenario of changing doctors or moving to a different city, an even greater majority—84 percent—said it would be important for them to have electronic copies of their medical records that they keep and control; and three-quarters of Americans are willing to share their personal information to help public officials look for disease outbreaks and research ways to improve the quality of health care if they have safeguards to protect their identity."[22]

The survey also shows that large majorities of Americans see a number of benefits from accessing their medical information online. Consumers say they want access to their medical information in order to ensure that it is accurate, to improve doctor-patient communications and to help prevent medical errors. "Ninety-one percent say it's important to review what their doctors write in their chart; 88 percent say online records would be important in reducing the number of unnecessary or repeated tests and procedures they undergo; …82 percent want to review test results online; and 84 percent would like to check for errors in their medical record."[22]

A 2006 survey of online adults' consumer preferences regarding health information technology reported, "77 percent would like to receive online reminders to visit their doctors; 74 percent would like to communicate with their doctors by email; 75 percent would like to schedule appointments online; 67 percent would like to receive the results of diagnostic tests via email; and 57 percent would like to use home monitoring devices, like blood pressure readings or blood tests, and send results to their doctors' offices by telephone or email."[16]

In an unpublished 2006 survey of a random selection of adult patients that had registered for a provider tethered PHR, an overwhelming majority of respondents (more than 85 percent in both cases) reported that they would like to complete pre-visit questionnaires online and view their results online, regardless of whether or not their provider had reviewed them.[23]

Americans also see ways in which they could gain more control over their healthcare by making use of personal health records: "…90 percent say it would be important to track their symptoms or changes in their health online; 83 percent of parents would be interested in using a network to track their child's health, such as tracking dates for immunizations; and 68 percent say having their information available online will give them more control over their own health care."[22]

A recent survey found that "U.S. adults favor providers (51 percent versus 17 percent) and insurance carriers (68 percent vs. 16 percent) who use electronic medical records over those who do not. While 12 percent of Americans currently review their personal medical records on their health insurance company's Web site, more than half say they would like to be able to check claims and coverage or access personal records electronically. Seventy-two percent of respondents view a computer system as more efficient than a paper system when it comes to managing medical records. A large 73 percent of Americans said they believe the benefits of electronic records, such as better care in emergences and reduction in medical errors, outweigh the potential privacy risks."[24]

The data in these surveys signifies the burgeoning desire that American healthcare consumers have in becoming empowered with regard to their healthcare. It also represents a shift from surveys done just a few years earlier pertaining to interest in PHRs. As there are more PHR offerings available and more direct-to-consumer marketing providing information about PHRs, the demand should continue to grow.

This chapter has reviewed some surveys and reports on PHRs that are available in the medical literature and the lay press. It is anticipated that PHRs will have a significant positive influence on healthcare. However, with limited data available regarding consumer and provider adoption of the various PHR models and their effects, further research is necessary to determine the impact that PHRs will ultimately have.

REFERENCES

1. Halamka JD, Mandl KD, Tang PC, et al. Early experiences with personal health records. *J Am Med Inform Assoc.* 2008; 15:1-7.
2. Liederman, et al. Patient-physician Web messaging: The impact on message volume and satisfaction. *J Gen Intern Med.* 2005; 20:52-57.
3. Miller HD. Unpublished study by the author. 2005.
4. Liberles C. Hearings on Personal Health Records; Meeting Minutes. National Health Information Infrastructure (NHII) Workgroup. National Committee on

Vital and Health Statistics, Department of Health and Human Services. January 5-6, 2005. Washington, DC.

5. Greene L. PHRs for Healthcare Consumers. E-Survey of the Month. Industry Pulse from the Healthcare Intelligence Network. HIN.com. May, 2008.

6. The Natural Marketing Institute. *The Boomer/Health Aging Database, 2006.* Harleysville, PA.

7. Medina K, Migliaccio J. *77 Truths about Marketing to the 50+ Consumer, Second Edition.* 2004. CD Publications.

8. Monali, et al. Drug reimportation practices in the United States. *Therpeutics and Clinical Risk Management.* 2007: 3(1):41-46.

9. Manos D. Leavitt predicts "Travelocity" system for healthcare pricing. *Healthcare IT News.* September 26, 2007.

10. Mangione CM, Damberg C, Horst M, Castles A, Kahn K. *UCLA/PBGS Medical Group and IPA Survey of Financial and Organizational Structure: Final Report.* San Francisco, CA: Pacific Business Group on Health; March 2000.

11. Agency for Healthcare Research and Quality, National CAHPS Benchmarking Database. *2007 CAHPS Hospital Survey Chartbook: What Patients Say about Their Experiences with Hospital Care.* Rockville, MD. Available at: https://www.cahps.ahrq.gov/content/ncbd/PDF/Hcahps_Chartbook_2007.pdf. Accessed June 12, 2008.

12. Harris Interactive. Consumer Backlash against Managed Care and Pharmaceutical Industries—Bottomed out or in Remission? May 29, 2001; 1(17).

13. Harris Poll Shows Number of "Cyberchondriacs" – Adults Who Have Ever Gone Online for Health Information– Increases to an Estimated 160 Million Nationwide. *The Harris Poll®* #76, July 31, 2007.

14. Miller H, Vandenbosch B, Ivanov D, Black P. Determinants of personal health record use: A large population study at Cleveland Clinic. *JHIM.* 2007; 21(3): 44-48.

15. Harris Interactive. Two in Five Adults Keep Personal or Family Health Records and Almost Everybody Thinks This Is a Good Idea. August 10, 2004. Available at: http://www.harrisinteractive.com/news/allnewsbydate.asp?NewsID=832. Accessed June 12, 2008.

16. Harris Interactive Poll: The Benefits of Electronic Medical Records Sound Good, but Privacy Could Become a Difficult Issue. February 8, 2007.

17. American Viewpoint, Lake Research Partners, Markle Foundation Connecting for Health. Survey Finds Americans Want Electronic Personal Health Information to Improve Own Health Care. November 11-15, 2006.

18. Mandl K, Kohane I. Tectonic shifts in the health information economy. Sounding Board. *NEJM.* 2008; 358:1732-1737.

19. Connecting for Health Common Framework. www.connnectingforhealth.org, June 2008.

20. Harris Interactive. Health-care Professionals, Pharmacies, Hospitals Gain the Public's Top Trust. January 28, 2004. Available at: http://www.harrisinteractive.com/news/allnewsbydate.asp?NewsID=749. Accessed June 12, 2008.
21. Bright B. Benefits of electronic health records seen as outweighing the privacy risks. *WSJ Online.* November 29, 2007. Available at: http://online.wsj.com/public/article_print/SB119565244262500549.html. Accessed June 12, 2008.
22. Connecting for Health Markle Foundation Press Release. Americans See Access to Their Medical Information as a Way to Improve Quality, Reduce Health Care Costs. December 6, 2006. Available at: http://www.connectingforhealth.org/news/pressrelease_120606.html.
23. Miller H. Other data; unpublished study. 2006.
24. Monegain B. Americans prefer digital medical records, survey shows. *Healthcare IT News.* May 2, 2007.

CHAPTER 6

PHR Architectures

In the context of information systems (IS), architecture is the system design. It describes where information is located, how it is captured and stored, and the mechanisms for retrieving and displaying it when and where needed. Information architecture delineates how information moves through a system—indicating who supplies it, who uses it and how functions are performed (e.g., ensuring that information quality is achieved). Like blueprints in the construction industry, it presents a picture of what the system will "look" like and communicates an understanding of how it operates. An architecture diagram will show all the data flows, processing and storage elements of a system. Most importantly, it provides a high-level description of how the functions of the system are realized. For each function, it should be possible to show details of how the function is implemented by tracing the sources of data, processes required and outputs needed.

Information architecture is important because it describes, and therefore determines, system functionality. The first step in evaluating whether a proposed system design will meet the requirements of the users is to assess the architecture. It should be possible to show how each requirement is met using specific paths through the architecture diagram. Since it describes the workflow and information flow, the architecture determines the interfaces and standards needed for implementation. In addition, architecture has a major impact on system performance and cost.

Some design options may result in poor performance due to processing and communications overloads. Alternatively, unnecessary system costs may result from resource expenditures to overcome these overloads. The cost impacts may be in the startup phase (related to initial investments required to implement the system) or the operational phase (involving staffing or other ongoing expenses) or both. The architecture may also play a role in determining the allocation of costs by, for example, distributing certain processing tasks (and by implication, their associated costs) to specific organizations. Just as you would not hire a building contractor without having first carefully reviewed and approved the blueprints, IS architecture must be carefully and thoroughly planned and reviewed by all stakeholders prior to the initiation of deployment activities.

REQUIREMENTS

Definition and Importance

Before discussing architecture for any system, the requirements must be known. An easy way to think about requirements is to ask the question, "What is it that will be possible to do when the system is complete that cannot be done now?" Clearly, any proposed architecture must satisfy the requirements by implementing the functions they describe via the new system. In the context of an IS, requirements represent the "destination." Just as a journey cannot meaningfully begin without a destination, IS development cannot start without requirements. This does not mean that the original requirements are never subject to change. Just as your destination can be changed after you begin a trip, requirements can be revised after system development has begun. However, just as changing the destination of a trip may mean that all or part of the initial journey may have been in the wrong direction, changing requirements nearly always means adding both time and cost to IS development.

PHR Requirements: Complete Health Records

In the context of PHRs, the key requirement is securely providing complete health records for each person whenever and wherever needed. Partial health records are of limited value, particularly if the missing sections are random. Reasonable health decisions are only possible if complete information is available. For example, if one medication is missing, then it is not possible to correctly assess the potential problems that may be caused by a new prescription. Also, the available information must be reliable or at least the source of each item must be known.

Optimally, clinicians should have complete and trustworthy information in a clinical IS for the technology to be the most useful and for the clinician to be able to deliver the highest quality and safety of care. As previously discussed, for information from sources external to the clinician's HIT system to be most useful, the information must be labeled with regard to the source and integrated (in a "push" fashion) into the clinician's workflow. More complete information would also decrease healthcare costs. Not knowing the results of previous tests and studies often results in duplication of those tests. Eliminating duplicate tests not only reduces healthcare costs but also the discomfort and inconvenience experienced by the healthcare consumer.

Electronic Information

Another important requirement is for all the information to be electronic. This is essential to allow health records to be rapidly delivered when and where needed. In fact, it is this ability to move electronic information rapidly that provides much of its value. While paper records can theoretically be scanned and the images transmitted easily, such data is not "computable" (i.e., it cannot be used easily by a computer.) For the data to be computable, it needs to be entered into a system electronically as discrete data. Non-discrete data not only makes it difficult to provide decision support, but also prevents the organization from displaying the information in formats that are useful to clinicians and healthcare consumers. For example, the value of a lab test over time may be of great interest (e.g., blood sugar in a diabetic). But a scanned paper record of a test result typically cannot be included in a trend display since the computer cannot interpret the contents of the scanned image.

At the present time, the major gap in electronic information for patients is the lack of EMRs in physician offices. While estimates vary, it is clear that no more than 20 percent of clinicians use EMRs in their practice. Since there are over 30 outpatient encounters for every hospital admission, this means that the vast majority of health records are still paper-based.[1] Before it can be possible to deliver complete health records when and where needed, it is critical that all physicians have EMRs so that the records are electronic.

As previously noted, payor-based ePHRs provide a wealth of patient information, at least with regard to the payor claims data. The transition for all providers to use EMRs, and then for all of these EMRs to be able to provide interfaced data to other systems in an integrated fashion, may require a substantial time period. However, providers are already required to submit claims data to the payor. If the payor, not the provider, is the healthcare constituent providing the individual with their health information through a payor-based ePHR, the information stream to the patient is not through the provider and the provider is bypassed. Although claims-based ePHRs may assist in care quality, delivery and consumer compliance as a bridge until true comprehensive interoperable PHRs are developed, such an information flow has the potential for the provider to become disenfranchised because the information flow is around rather than through them. In addition, though the claims data more accurately reflects patient behavior (unless the patient is paying for their care out of pocket), it does not necessarily accurately reflect provider behavior. The provider may have ordered medications, tests or studies with which the patient has elected not to comply. Finally, claims data by its very nature does not fully reflect the details of the clinical encounter and patient care.

Stakeholder Cooperation

Another key requirement to provide complete health records is for all stakeholders to cooperate in supplying their records. Although physicians, hospitals, labs, imaging centers and insurance companies all realize that everyone would benefit from having more complete patient records, they may be reluctant to voluntarily participate in a system unless they can be sure that all their peers will also do so. In addition, each group has, to a varying degree, proprietary interests with respect to their records. In particular, there is an understandable reluctance to share information with "competitors."

In this environment, mandates or significant incentives could guide cooperation for the essential provision of information from all stakeholders. While seeking a new mandate or designing a significant incentive program is a long and difficult process at either the state or federal level, the current HIPAA regulations provide an existing requirement that can be invoked to address this problem. HIPAA specifically provides that patients must be given copies of their records upon request, with virtually no exceptions. While such copies may not be electronic and holders of information are allowed to assess "reasonable fees" for the copies, it turns out that one practical effect of this HIPAA rule is to mandate stakeholder participation in a patient-centric system if the consumer wants to populate a PHR. Faced with large numbers of patient-authorized requests for copies of records, it is most economical for healthcare stakeholders to provide electronic versions. Furthermore, the knowledge that all the other stakeholders will be required to do likewise helps to eliminate reluctance to participate. At that point, charging fees to patients for records becomes counterproductive to the interest of each stakeholder. As long as everyone participates, the most complete information for each patient will be ensured. Such charges would also be viewed very negatively by the public, leading to undesirable negative press reports about any institution or group that imposed them.

Financial Sustainability

As will be discussed in Chapter 9, any PHR system must be financially sustainable to survive. This requires ongoing revenues that more than cover expenses. Potential sources for operating funds include government, healthcare stakeholders, employers, insurers, and consumers. At the present time, it appears that consumers are the most likely reliable source of continuing revenue. Governments are strapped for funds at all levels and are typically uninterested in providing operational funds for any new activity as a matter of policy. While healthcare providers do benefit from the availability of ePHRs, there is no easy mechanism to fund this using the existing reimbursement system given that it does not provide payment for such services. Additionally, providers would be reluctant to fund an un-tethered ePHR that does not bind the consumer to their practice or healthcare system. Employers and insurers could, and do, pay for these systems, as some of the direct financial benefits accrue to them.

However, consumers consistently indicate a willingness to pay for such systems, provided they contain their EMRs. Many consumers understand that today no one has access to their complete medical records and that such access can be extremely valuable in ensuring that they receive the proper care. In a 2005 survey, 52 percent of consumers nationwide indicated a willingness to pay $5/month or more for their medical records to be electronic.[2] In a follow-up survey in 2007, 51 percent of consumers said they would pay "a reasonable price" for this service.[3] Clearly, to engage consumers, the system must provide real value for them and the monthly cost must be modest.

As previously discussed, employers are offering incentives to their employees to adopt healthier behaviors as well as disincentives for persistent uncontrolled medical conditions or continued engagement in unhealthy behaviors. Employees motivated by such financial incentives and disincentives could reap financial benefits by using an ePHR that included tools to help them to achieve their behavioral or care management goals.

In thinking about possible groups of consumers that would immediately be willing to subscribe to such a system, there are at least three good examples: (1) consumers with one or more chronic diseases who are currently collecting and carrying their records as they see one provider after another; (2) children of elderly parents who are managing their medical care for them; and (3) parents of young children, particularly a child with a chronic illness, who find it extremely difficult to maintain complete and accurate information about required immunizations, needed school physical exams and the child's schedule of doctor appointments and treatments. Undoubtedly, there are other groups who also would find immediate benefit.

Public Trust

Since medical records contain extremely sensitive and private information, public trust is essential in any effort to make these records more complete and more easily available. The public perceives that efforts to make health information electronic and accessible for care also increase the risk of misuse of both individual records and, through the power of information technology, huge numbers of records all at once. The multiple highly-publicized incidents relating to data loss have helped to increase public sensitivity. In consumer polls, concern about privacy is a key issue. For example, a 2005 Harris Interactive poll found that "Overall, the public is equally split with 48 percent (when told about electronic medical records) believing that the benefits outweigh the risks to privacy and 47 percent believing the risks outweigh the benefits."[4]

Earlier polls reveal that between 13 percent and 17 percent of consumers admit to "information hiding behavior" in healthcare (e.g., going to an alternate provider so their primary caregiver is not aware of the information).[5, 6] Given the natural reluctance of individuals to disclose the use of such tactics, it seems likely that this represents an underestimate of the actual number of consumers trying to protect their privacy in this manner.

The substantial minority concerned about privacy are not likely to participate if systems are built that are not trustworthy. They will either opt out (losing the benefits for themselves, as well as reducing the overall benefits possible with more complete population data) or actively oppose the systems politically. Neither of these outcomes is desirable and the latter could imperil the availability of ePHRs for everyone, so public trust is truly a key requirement.

Policies to address public trust must include at least three key elements: (1) patients must control the use of their own information; (2) organizations serving as information custodians must be trusted; and (3) the IS handling the information must have a trustworthy, secure and reliable architecture.

Patient Control of Information

The overriding requirement for public trust is to engage patients in the control of their own information. This provides a realistic and practical solution for privacy policy since each person can then establish whatever policy they wish and change it anytime they deem it necessary.[7] It is wishful thinking to believe that it is possible to develop a set of "universal" privacy policies that everyone (or even most people) could endorse. Even if such a task were possible, the resultant policies are likely to be so complex and voluminous as to defy easy understanding. More importantly, allowing each person to control their own information greatly reduces the trust level needed for the organization actually holding the information. Without patient control, the organization must be trusted not only to hold and safeguard the sensitive medical information (which is necessary in any case), but also to make independent decisions about its release. Such independent decisions, presumably made according to established (but complex) policies, would be subject to endless interpretation and challenge. With patients in control, the data holder is responsible only to follow instructions from each individual about data access and release. The latter is equivalent to the responsibility of financial banks to follow account-holder instructions about disbursements.

Consumer control of information would need to be associated with consumers' assuming responsibility for withholding information from providers. Deleting or withholding health information would provide only a partial record to the clinician, limiting the usefulness of the information and potentially creating adverse care events.

ePHRs could contain an "in case of emergency" (ICE) form that included basic critical health and contact information such as diagnoses, procedures, active medications, allergies, advanced directives, durable power of attorney and a list of providers. This form could be accessed by any provider in the event of an emergency. Alternatively, an ePHR could include a "break the glass" functionality that would allow a provider to access all of the individual's ePHR data in the case of an emergency. "Breaking the glass" would initiate an immediate audit trail for anyone accessing the information therein. This audit trail would automatically be made available to the individual to whom the information pertained.

ePHRs were not envisioned when the HIPAA regulations were written. Therefore, ePHRs or ePHR information platforms that are offered by third party vendors are not covered by the HIPAA regulations. However, publicly-available ePHRs are covered by the Stored Communications Act (United States Code Title 18 sections 2701 et seq). Under this federal law, an ePHR provider may not release any information to any private party without the consent of the subscriber (see Chapter 8). This is a higher level of protection than HIPAA that allows release of data without consent for treatment, payment and healthcare operations. Despite this legal protection, there is currently no oversight to ensure that these systems are actually complying with their own terms and conditions.

In addition, given that almost all Web site policies are included as terms and conditions, it is possible to check the "I agree" box without ever opening the terms and conditions. Most Web site terms and conditions are long and written in legalese at a highly sophisticated level of language. It is important for individuals to be able to make decisions about the release of their healthcare information; however, these decisions should be informed. It is recommended that:

- The public should be educated regarding the potential implications surrounding the exchange and usage of personal health information in the context of an ePHR.
- All ePHR products should clearly, simply and concisely list their security, privacy and data usage policies and make them available in a consumer friendly fashion.
- There should be disinterested third-party validation and periodic compliance audits to ensure the ePHR products' compliance with their stated policies. Once industry standards are established, ePHR products that are in compliance could receive a "seal of approval" to be prominently displayed at the consumer access point.

Trusted Organization

The organization holding electronic medical information must be trusted. The most obvious example of similar trusted organizations is financial banks—trust is important as they hold money on our behalf. However, trust in financial institutions does not flow from the frequent presence of "trust" in their names, but rather from federal and state regulations including required periodic audits to ensure transparency of operations and free, no co-pay, no deductible federal insurance for all depositors. Establishing a similar regulatory and audit framework for ePHRs to provide a solid basis for trust is highly desirable.

Absent such regulation, an independent multi-stakeholder, non-profit community organization may be able to function as the trusted entity in a local area. It would need to operate in an open, balanced and transparent manner and submit itself to independent privacy audits (the IS equivalent of financial audits).

Trusted Architecture

The final element in public trust is trustworthy system architecture. Two key threats must be minimized: (1) large-scale information loss and (2) individual record loss. There are many ways that such an architecture can be established. One such method is a two-server solution, with one server used for searches and the other for access to individual health records. To prevent unauthorized remote use, the searching server can be physically isolated from any connectivity and placed in an ultra-secure location. All data input and output would be via physical media (since there would be no electronic connections) carried into the server room, with meticulous audit trails. Personnel with access to the searching server would be carefully screened and monitored. No laptops or other electronic devices would be allowed in the facility.

The second server would be for individual health records. Since no searching across records would be supported, it could be specially configured to allow access to only one record at a time. This could be done with a version of Secure Linux that establishes which single record can be accessed upon login.[8] The operating system would then physically prevent access to any other record by that user by, for example, filtering the addresses of all disk access requests. Another method would be to place a complete copy of the authorized record in the user's address space upon login and completely disallow any access to the media that contains such records by users. Upon logout, any changes to the record would be written to disk by the operating system. In this manner, no system user would be able to access any information beyond a single health record. On a daily basis, all record updates could be written to media for transfer to the searching server.

TYPES OF PHR ARCHITECTURES

Standalone PHRs

The standalone PHR is not an ePHR model. As implied by the name, all of the data in this model is entered manually by the individual. Clearly, the individual is then responsible for the accuracy and completeness of the information. The data may be printed and carried with the individual, burned to a CD or loaded onto a "thumb drive" to give to their physician.

There is an inherent problem of information integrity with a self-entered architecture. While healthcare providers routinely rely on patients to provide information about symptoms, they will be understandably reluctant to base critical decisions on lab results or other objective data that has been entered by patients. To avoid misinformation due to transcribing or other errors, having directly entered information from original sources is essential. In addition, such "third party" information must be verifiably unchanged.

The other major problem of the self-entered model is the inconvenience and tedium associated with direct patient entry of all data. Because of this, it is unlikely that the record will be updated promptly. Also, even the most diligent consumer is highly likely to make numerous errors in the transcription of their medical information. While there are many available standalone PHR templates available for download to an individual's PC, their usage is light. This is undoubtedly due to the combination of extensive and continuing data entry requirements and the minimal benefits related to lack of provider use of "untrustworthy" information.

Tethered ePHRs

The tethered model is simply a window to the database of the healthcare constituent that is providing the tethered ePHR that allows the individual to view their own information (or portions of their own information) contained in this database. Tethered models generally include services; these services depend on what kind of healthcare constituent is offering the tethered ePHR. In the case of a provider, the services might include looking up personally relevant health information, appointment scheduling, prescription renewal and bill paying. In the tethered model, the data is generally not transportable or interoperable, and does not move out of the healthcare constituent's database that is providing the portal.

A tethered approach to ePHRs, wherein selective information is loaded automatically as it is generated, provides much greater value and eliminates the need for extensive consumer data entry. However, unless such a record is "tethered" to all possible data sources, its value will still be limited because it will be incomplete. In the current healthcare market, many healthcare constituents are reluctant to participate in such a multi-tethered model as their goal in offering an ePHR to their consumers is to tether the consumer to their organization.

However, with the advent of third party data repositories or "platforms" that seek to interface with tethered ePHRs and healthcare system EMRs to enable data transportability at the behest of the individual, this model has been altered to include the potential for tethered ePHR data exchange and interoperability.

Distributed ePHRs

In the distributed ePHR model (see Figure 6-1), data for a given person is left in the various databases where it is generated and only brought together when needed for care. Although this model is sometimes called "federated," that term is not used here because a "federated" database often implies control from a single point that functions much like a central repository.

In this model, there is a need to maintain at least a central index of where information can be found for a particular patient; without such an index, finding information about each patient would require a query to every possible source of medical information worldwide— clearly an impractical approach. The index would be used to generate queries to the locations where information is stored and the responses to those queries would be aggregated (in real time) to produce the patient's complete record. Whenever information about the patient was generated at a new site, the index would need to be updated to add that site to the list of record locations for that patient.

Figure 6-1. Distributed PHR Model

(In response to a patient-authorized inquiry to an index of where patients have records, secondary queries to all the record locations are generated (which may be numerous). After waiting for responses from all the other health IS holding records, the comprehensive records for the patient are assembled in real time and delivered to the site of care. After the patient encounter, the new data is entered into the clinician's EHR system and another pointer is added to the index. The next time the patient presents for care, the previous EHR system will be queried along with all the other prior locations where data for that patient is stored.)

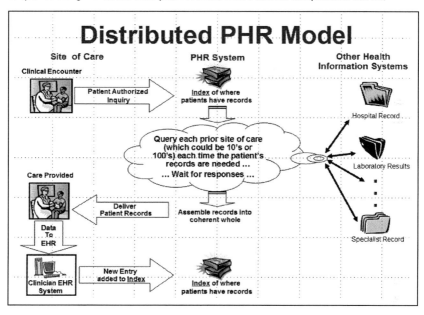

While a distributed model has been advocated as an approach to ePHR architecture,[9] it has several very serious disadvantages. First, the response time for a distributed system would be slow. For each patient, it would depend on the response time of the slowest system that had data for that person. In addition, time would be needed to transmit all the information for the patient each time it was requested. Since many patients have substantial amounts of data at multiple places, a response time of at least several seconds is likely. The model requires unattainable levels of reliability to ensure complete records. If any source of information for a given patient is not available, then a complete record cannot be obtained. Since thousands of systems might be involved in providing such information, chances are that some of them will be inoperative or unresponsive at any given time. Such a system would be extremely expensive: every system would need to have additional hardware, software and communications capabilities to be able to respond to queries. In addition, there would need to be a costly "network central" operations center that was staffed to monitor and troubleshoot all the systems around the clock to ensure that they were online and operational. Every connected system would need to be fully interoperable in real time to allow rapid fetching and assembly of records. Since a given patient could receive care anywhere in the world, this interoperability would need to be widespread.

The data that could successfully be retrieved and exchanged might also be limited to discrete data to which national or international standards apply, due to the lack of standards for a common data vocabulary, common data model, data normalization or metadata tagging.

The distributed model also exposes health records to additional security risks since they are transmitted twice every time they are requested (once from the source to the distributed system hub and a second time to the end user).

Finally, the distributed model does not allow practical searching across patient records. A search would require the records to be retrieved one-by-one and then analyzed to see if the search criteria are met. Such a sequential search would be unbelievably slow and consume huge amounts of computing power of every system that had information on the population being searched. For example, if the average retrieval and analysis time for each record was just one second (a reasonable estimate given the requirement for a query/response cycle to numerous external systems for each patient), each search of one million records would take about 12 days.

Given these serious drawbacks, it is not surprising that many of the RHIOs that have been created based on the distributed model are failing.[10]

Central

In the central repository ePHR architecture (see Figure 6-2), all data for a given patient is kept in a single location, analogous to a financial bank account. This model requires healthcare constituent's health IS to be interfaced with the central repository. At each episode of care, the information in the patient's account, from the central repository, can be available to the provider; any new information generated (from any source) is immediately deposited into that same account. In this way, the information is always up-to-date and available.

Figure 6-2. Central PHR Model

(In response to a patient-authorized inquiry, the patient's records are immediately retrieved from the central repository and delivered to the site of care. After the patient encounter, the new information is entered into the clinician's EHR system and also sent to the central repository. Next time the patient needs care, the central repository will have all the records without the need to retrieve data from any other health IS.)

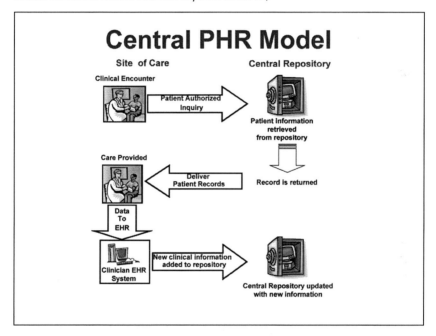

In contrast to the distributed model, the central approach is lower cost and has numerous other advantages. The response time is immediate since all the information is directly available in each patient's account. Reliability is only dependent on the status of the central system, which would include all the backup and fail-safe mechanisms needed for extremely high availability. Since each source of health information need only deposit new information into the central account once, expensive queries to the source systems every time the information is needed are avoided. Given that the central system would only need to monitor itself, the high costs of monitoring all connected health IS required for the distributed model would be avoided. A single data normalization standard could be developed and each deposit can be verified for content and either "normalized" or rejected/returned for clarification if it cannot be properly interpreted. Such data normalization would allow for trending of data. Systems that are not interoperable could send images of documents for storage in the central system until they are able to achieve content interoperability. Security is better with a central repository since the location of all information is known and can be protected with stringent measures. Also, when a patient record is needed, the information is only transmitted once—back to the end user. Audits conducted to ensure that the standards of privacy and security are met can be conducted on a single system rather than all of the systems in a distributed model. Finally, searching the data is easy and fast since it is all present in the central repository and its content can be indexed (much like creating an index for a book that lists page numbers where given words can be found).

As noted above, several communities that have implemented an operational health information infrastructure have utilized the central repository model. However, no community as of this writing provides patient access and control over the distribution of these records, or an ePHR.

The central model includes third party repositories. Recently, both Google[11] and Microsoft[12] have announced secure, patient-controlled repositories for health information. Also, a consortium of large employers led by Intel and Wal-Mart has been pursuing a central ePHR repository for their employees, known as Dossia.[13] These efforts have previously been discussed and share a clear recognition that a central repository of lifelong medical records is needed to improve the quality and efficiency of healthcare. The principle that access to such a repository must be controlled by the patient has also been clearly acknowledged and supported.

However, these initiatives must overcome at least two key challenges: (1) earning and maintaining the trust of the individuals who use the system and (2) populating the repository directly from authoritative healthcare sources.

The revenue model for systems such as Google and Microsoft is primarily focused on advertising. It has previously been noted that transparent provider quality, outcomes and cost information with tools on selecting providers and healthcare organizations that are centers of excellence will encourage individuals to make better and more informed choices. Healthcare advertising may be the antithesis of this goal, even if it is controlled by existing healthcare advertising regulations. Targeted marketing to an individual with a specific health condition to market healthcare goods and services that are not based on quality, outcomes and experience could be counterproductive to ePHR goals. The need for some form of regulation and oversight of third party health data repositories has previously been discussed.

Finally, none of these ePHR models address the need to make all the information electronic in the first place by providing incentives to outpatient providers to acquire and use EMR systems in their offices in order to have complete, longitudinal ePHRs. The ultimate success of ePHR health information repositories will depend on their ability to successfully address this critical issue.

PERFECT IS THE ENEMY OF THE GOOD

PHR development, implementations and adoption are rapidly evolving. The ideal PHR model is one which includes not only the comprehensive health information pertaining to the individual, but all the necessary tools for that individual to best manage their health and wellness.

Given the current state of the evolution of health IS in the U.S., this ideal model continues to be elusive. Most of the care delivered in this country is still documented on paper. When it is documented electronically, healthcare constituents are neither inclined nor incented to share the information with their competitors and some continue to be reluctant to share the information with their consumers. Slowly evolving attitudes, market forces, consumer demand and changes in the healthcare system itself may lead to the enablement of the ideal ePHR model. In the interim, however, there is still much good that can come from any of the ePHR models that have been discussed.

For example, complete information, while ideal, may not necessarily lead to dramatically improved healthcare outcomes:

access to relevant information is necessary to move towards this goal. Dramatic improvements in utilization, treatment, and outcomes have been seen when physicians in emergency department settings are given a PBHR—while decidedly incomplete, it is still full of useful information. That record shows recent patient encounters, filled prescriptions, completed diagnostic and laboratory tests, diagnoses and treatments. One study demonstrated that when hospitals and physicians had a PBHR available to them, they provided more focused and informed care and actually billed more accurately, thus increasing the revenue per case and reducing unreimbursed costs. The health plan involved saved over $450 per encounter.[13]

To halt the progress of ePHR development while waiting for HIT and healthcare policy in the U.S. to evolve would not only be a mistake—perfect being the enemy of good—but would also be impossible. As the various ePHR models progress, there are continuous feature and function enhancements that will ultimately be incorporated in all ePHRs and will assist with accomplishing the goals of these systems and technologies.

REFERENCES

1. Accenture. Majority of Consumers Believe Electronic Medical Records Can Improve Medical Care, Accenture Survey Finds. Press release. July 20, 2005. Available at: accenture.tekgroup.com/article_display.cfm?article_id=4236 . Accessed July 17, 2008.
2. Accenture. Consumers See Electronic Health Records as Important Factor When Choosing a Physician and Are Willing to Pay for Service. Accenture Research. February 27, 2007. Available at: http://newsroom.accenture.com/article_display. cfm?article_id=4509 . Accessed June 12, 2008.
3. Bright B. Benefits of electronic health records seen as outweighing privacy risks. *WSJ Online*. November 29, 2007. Available at http://online.wsj.com/article/ SB119565244262500549.html. Accessed June 12, 2008.
4. Harris Interactive. Health Information Privacy (HIPAA) notices have improved public's confidence that their medical information is being handled properly. February 24, 2005. Available at: http://www.harrisineractive.com/news/ allnewsbydate.asp?NewsID=894. Accessed June 12, 2008.
5. California Health Care Foundation. National consumer health privacy survey 2005. November 2005. Available at: http://www.chcf.org/topics/view. cfm?itemID=115694. Accessed March 23, 2008.

6. Harris Interactive. Many U.S. adults are satisfied with use of their personal health records. March 26, 2007. Available at: http://www.harrisinteractive.com/harris_poll/index.asp?PID=743. Accessed June 12, 2008.

7. Halamka JD, Mandl KD, Tang PC. Early experiences with personal health records. *J Am Med Inf Assoc.* 2008; 15:1-7.

8. National Security Agency. Security-enhanced Linux. Available at: http://www.nsa.gov/selinux/. Accessed June 12, 2008.

9. Markle Foundation. Available at: http://www.connectingforhealth.org/resources/final_phwg_report1.pdf . Accessed March 23, 2008.

10. Freid BM. Gauging the Progress of the National Health Information Technology Initiative: Perspectives from the Field. California Health Care Foundation, 2008. Available at http://www.chcf.org/topics/view.cfm?itemID=133553 . Accessed March 23, 2008.

11. Hamilton DP. Google Health's Cleveland pilot program – and the nagging questions it doesn't come close to answering. *VentureBeat.* February 21, 2008. Available at: http://venturebeat.com/2008/02/21/the-nagging-questions-raised-by-google-healths-cleveland-testbed/. Accessed June 12, 2008.

12. Hamilton DP. Microsoft launches HealthVault to manage your health search and medical records – but it will hurt a bit. *VentureBeat.* October 4, 2007. Available at: http://venturebeat.com/2007/10/04/microsoft-launches-healthvault-its-bid-to-manage-your-health-records/. Accessed June 12, 2007.

13. Dossia home page. Available at: http://www.dossia.org/home. Accessed June 12, 2008.

14. Enrado P. Payer-based summaries paying off. *Healthcare IT News.* September 27, 2007. Available at www.healthcareitnews.com/story.cms?id=7812. Accessed October 14, 2008.

CHAPTER 7

Planning and Implementation of Healthcare Constituent-Based PHRs: Some Practical Considerations

In the previous chapters, we have clearly identified a PHR model that is healthcare-consumer controlled, electronic, interoperable, transportable, comprehensive, secure and private. This model is difficult to achieve given current HIT capabilities. The reality of the current HIT landscape is that systems:

- Have not implemented uniform data standards, making data exchange difficult; and
- Do not have important data electronically available as many systems and/or implementations of these systems do not store valuable data in a discrete or reusable form.

These factors add to the difficulty, time and expense of building the required interfaces between systems using Health Level Seven (HL7) and other data exchange "languages" as well as the scope of the data that is retrievable and the usefulness of this data. "Health Level Seven is one of several American National Standards Institute (ANSI)

-accredited Standards Developing Organizations (SDOs) operating in the healthcare arena."[1] The HL7 organization develops the standards for healthcare data exchange by creating standard protocols or specifications that allow disparate HIT systems to exchange healthcare data.

The reality of the current HIT adoption landscape is that:

- Most clinicians are not using EMRs.
- The vast majority of healthcare enterprises that have implemented EMRs do not exchange data beyond their enterprise.
- Few if any of the RHIOs developed to date have fundamentally included a PHR.
- The data for other healthcare constituents such as payors, pharmacies and others also generally exist as silos—therefore, it is difficult to aggregate data in a PHR, particularly due to the constraints of limited health data standards facilitating the exchange of complex clinical or behavioral data.

It may well be that without a "big bang" change in healthcare or HIT, the PHR landscape will continue to evolve as it has been with diverse PHR offerings all with limited data, but none containing an individual's longitudinal comprehensive information. As previously mentioned, PHR platforms or changes in community approaches to HIT system architecture may facilitate this evolution.

Healthcare consumers' attitudes towards healthcare delivery and PHRs are also continuing to evolve. Surveys of consumers using PHRs have demonstrated that the primary influence on consumers' PHR adoption is their physician's recommendation.

Clinicians continue to be concerned that PHRs may mean an increased workload for them. Providers may embrace PHRs if they:

- Are reimbursed for their time spent interacting with the patient or reviewing patient information through the PHR.
- Utilize a PHR that integrates the information from the PHR (appropriately source and date/time stamped) into their own EMR, in a "push" to the provider rather than requiring the provider to "pull" the information to them. For example, if a provider is viewing results from outside their health system, these results would need to appear in the same section of their EMR as a result from within their system and in the appropriate

chronological or reverse chronological sequence. All external results or information would be marked with the source.

- Are able to download some of the documentation burden to the patient through the PHR. For example, a clinician pushes a pre-visit questionnaire or other information form to a patient prior to the visit through a PHR. The patient completes the form and "pushes" it back from the PHR to the clinician's EMR right into the clinician's EMR visit template. The physician then uses this template as the basis for the note that she or he will complete when face-to-face with the patient. In this example, part of the burden of clinical documentation has actually been transferred to the patient. In addition, templates could be designed that would capture the data entered as discrete data. This scenario becomes increasingly feasible as companies promote HIT mapping tools. These products have mapped standard clinical language to commonly used and lay friendly terms. Using such tools a patient may complete a form with lay friendly terms for their diagnoses or family history, and the mapping could enable the proper clinical term in the EMR for the physician to review.

Such a scenario is already feasible in a tethered PHR. In many implementations of tethered PHRs, physicians also control what information is released to the patient, or the timing of when the information is released to the patient, or both. In addition, the physician could include a message with the result. This control makes these systems more palatable to physicians who are concerned about being inundated with patient's questions regarding their results.

Provider-tethered and payor-tethered ePHRs are implemented by many organizations and are widely available. Implementing the provider-tethered ePHR raises unique challenges for the HIT professional. There are two distinct constituency groups, the providers and the patients and their interests in the ePHR features and functions may be quite different, if not opposed. For example, frequently providers are reluctant to allow patients to see all of their results or diagnoses, whereas patients want immediate access to this information regardless of whether or not the provider has seen it.[2]

For those in the industry that will be implementing such systems in the near future, this chapter serves as a rough guideline for some practical considerations for the implementation of a PHR project.

INITIAL PROJECT PLANNING AND BUDGETING

Clearly the project plan and budget will depend on your particular project. The following represents a starter set of questions to help you begin to scope, plan and budget your project.

- Make or buy?
    - ❑ If your PHR is tethered, this implies an existing EMR in your organization.
        - If your EMR is licensed from a vendor, does the vendor have a PHR product that you can implement?
            - Is there an additional charge, and if so what is the charge structure? For example, would you pay a license fee per patient?
        - Does the project involve attempting to interface a third party product into your existing EMR?
            - Does your organization have staff with the required skills to accomplish this or will this need to be outsourced?
        - Are you developing an ePHR to be interfaced to an existing EMR?
            - If you are developing the PHR, will you use internal resources or outsource the development of:
                - ❑ The features and functions document?
                - ❑ The use cases?
                - ❑ The code?
                - ❑ Who will own the intellectual property of the PHR?
- In-house or outsource?
    - If you are developing an ePHR project, are you hiring a full-time Web administrator(s) to configure your ePHR system or engaging consultants to do this work?
    - Are you planning to internally host the system's servers or will you have these remote hosted?
- What is the privacy and security model?

- ❏ Will your security include a demilitarized zone (DMZ) model (this refers to a model of server security) and, if so, will this be internal to your organization or remote hosted?
- ❏ Will you be using email, without personal health information contained therein, to let patients know when there is something new for them in the ePHR?
- ❏ Will the privacy and security technical and implementation model meet the standards required in HIPAA?
- Interfaces
  - ❏ Does the project scope include only the data in the EMR or will you also need to interface to separate billing, admission discharge transfer (ADT) or other systems?
  - ❏ Will you interface directly to pharmacies for patients to request prescription refills?
  - ❏ Will you interface to other healthcare constituents, e.g. if you are a provider organization interface to payors?
  - ❏ Will you interface to a PHR platform?
- Marketing considerations
  - ❏ What do you want to call the product?
  - ❏ Is your proposed name available for trademark?
  - ❏ Have you investigated if the related URL(s) are available for purchase?
  - ❏ How will you incorporate the product into your overall marketing brand strategy?
  - ❏ How extensive is your marketing plan and what marketing budget do you need?
  - ❏ Who will develop the text for the site?
    - Site FAQs?
    - Context specific help?
  - ❏ What marketing collateral do you need to develop?
  - ❏ Will you develop an ePHR demo available on your Web site?
    - If you have a licensed ePHR, does your vendor allow this?
  - ❏ What is the marketing communication plan?
  - ❏ Will you need to pay the participants in your advisory groups or focus groups for their time?
  - ❏ Will you be mailing surveys? Using online surveys?
  - ❏ What educational and training materials do you need?

- ❏ How will you track patient satisfaction with the system?
- Deployment and staffing considerations
  - ❏ Are you implementing the project in multiple phases or in a single phase?
  - ❏ Will you pilot the PHR to a small population (such as employees) before rolling out to the general public? (This is recommended!)
  - ❏ How many patients are you planning to sign up over what period of time?
  - ❏ What are your project staffing considerations?
  - ❏ How many support staff and clinicians will you need to train?
  - ❏ Will you need additional help desk staff?
  - ❏ Will you need to hire special help desk staff as these calls will be coming from patients and not employees?
  - ❏ Will your PHR require participation and training of both clinical and administrative staff?
- Legal Considerations
  - ❏ Do you have in-house legal resources that you will be using or will you need to budget for some legal consulting time?
- Features and Functions
  - ❏ What are the final features and function sets that will be included in the project?
    - Will you be rolling out features and functions in phases?
  - ❏ Are you implementing proxy access?
    - How will you process access for individuals with healthcare durable power of attorney?
    - How will you handle adolescents?
  - ❏ Will your system allow for e-visits?
    - Will you charge for e-visits?
    - Will you charge for patients to message their physicians?
  - ❏ How will patients sign up for the system?
    - Online
    - In person
    - User ID and password sent by U.S. mail for initial log on?
  - ❏ Will you have on-site support to help them log in for the first time?

- ❏ Does your organization's scheduling practices and scheduling system allow you to build direct scheduling through the ePHR?
  - If so, do you want to use existing appointment types or create special "ePHR" appointments?
  - What is the time period to hold an "ePHR" appointment open until it would revert to a normal available appointment?
- ❏ Will patients be receiving alerts and reminders through the system?
  - If so, what will be your governance process to determine the patient alerts and reminders?
  - Are the alerts automated or does the provider need to push them to the individual?
- ❏ Will you be providing links to educational materials within the PHR?
  - Does your organization create patient educational materials providing an in-house source?
  - Does this in-house source provide sufficient content to cover all of the materials needed in the PHR?
  - If you currently have a contract with a vendor to supply patient educational materials for your public Web site, does the contract permit linkage through a PHR or will you need to renegotiate the contract?
  - How will you link the materials to be context sensitive in your PHR?
  - If you do not use an automated search, how will you maintain these links?
  - Does your PHR contain a content linking and maintenance function?
- ❏ Are you implementing prescription renewal and appointment scheduling requests
  - If you are, how will you set up and maintain the eMailboxes for the end users to receive these requests?
- Benchmarking
  - ❏ Are you planning to calculate return on investment or internal rate of return?

- If so, do you have the necessary current benchmark data?
- What data will you need from the system to calculate the above?

• Reports
  - ❏ Will you establish time goals for handling appointment requests, billing queries, prescription renewal requests, etc?
  - ❏ What reports will you need from the system to track compliance with these goals?

These questions and more will need to be considered to create your initial project plan and budget.

CHANGE MANAGEMENT CONSIDERATIONS: WHO IS YOUR PROJECT SPONSOR? WHO ARE YOUR CONSTITUENTS? HOW WILL YOU CREATE THEIR "BUY-IN"?

In the environment of a provider-tethered ePHR, the needs and wants of several constituencies will need to be addressed: the clinicians, the support staff and the patients. Clinicians continue to be apprehensive that an ePHR will cause them to be flooded with work and some continue to be reluctant to give up the practice of paternalistic medicine. They are concerned that patients will message them incessantly, or that they will be swamped with questions regarding interpretation of the patients' results both resulting in increased work. In fact, a study about patient–provider Web messaging published in 2005 demonstrated the opposite: "Results showed that physicians using the electronic media to communicate had about a ten percent increase in productivity."[3]

In some environments where provider-tethered ePHRs have been implemented, providers actually continue to manually release results to patients despite the fact that this represents more work for them than automated release.

Patients, on the other hand, want to have all of their health information available to them and to use the Internet to fill in the information gaps. Most PHRs include the ability to have context-sensitive, institutionally defined links to trusted health information from the Internet. Links to provider-endorsed, layperson-friendly health information will facilitate consumers' ability to understand the information in their ePHR.

Given these constituency positions, one of the first suggestions in the implementation of a PHR is to organize a strong, respected organizational leader or leaders to be the sponsor(s) and to deliver frequent messages regarding the project to create internal buy-in. To create constituency buy-in, the creation of two separate advisory counsels is recommended—one composed of representatives of all of the internal groups that will be affected by the project (e.g., physicians, nurses, schedulers, front desk, call center) and the other composed of patients. These groups can function not only to help determine the features and functions of the ePHR to be implemented and provide feedback on usability, but also to become project advocates throughout their greater constituency communities. For both constituency groups to have broader input as well as to generate excitement and anticipation of the project, online and mail surveys are useful, as is frequent project communication. The sponsor selection, advisory groups, surveys and communication plans need to be incorporated into the overall project plan and timeline and should be assigned adequate resources determined during the planning stages of the project. The sponsorship, advisory groups and projects communications should continue throughout the life of the project.

BUILD, TEST, TRAIN, PILOT, EVALUATE, ROLL OUT, OPTIMIZE

Once the initial project scope has been determined and the project plan/timeline has been developed, these phases proceed much like any other HIT project. The better prepared and more involved your constituents are from the beginning of the project, the smoother the project roll out.

ADDITIONAL SUGGESTIONS AND CONSIDERATIONS

Tracking Online Services (Reporting Considerations)

Often with the features and functions you might be implementing within an ePHR, there are immediate reporting requirements that will affect consumer adoption of the system and its offered services. If a patient attempts to schedule an appointment or renew a prescription from the PHR and the consumer expectations (which hopefully have been set as part of the marketing campaign) are not met, the consumer may not trust the system again for such services, defeating the purpose of your well-planned project. To begin to identify and then create the reports that you will need to ensure that your organization is meeting consumer expectations, you may be required to create use cases with elaborate workflow diagrams and Web site story boards. This is particularly true when you need to understand what data is required to build a report that will enable you to track the success of your project.

Here is a detailed example to illustrate the concept: If a patient tries to use the ePHR to request an appointment and is frustrated by the process, they will be more likely to pick up the phone and call the organization the next time they want to make an appointment or even make the appointment elsewhere. The system should provide an easy-to-use interface and the organization should set a timeline goal for the patient to receive a response. A report will then need to be developed such that all outcomes of appointment requests can be tracked and assigned to an individual or a pool of individuals so that the manager can follow up to ensure that quality goals are met. There are several possible outcomes for an appointment request:

- The appointment is scheduled as requested and the patient receives a message informing them of the outcome within 24 hours of the request that was made by the patient.
- The appointment is scheduled as requested and the patient does not receive a message informing them of the outcome or receives the message in a time frame that is greater than 24 hours.
- The appointment cannot be scheduled as requested and the patient receives a message informing them of the outcome within 24 hours of the request that was made by the patient.
- The appointment cannot be scheduled as requested and the patient does not receive a message informing them of the outcome or receives the message in a time frame that is greater than 24 hours.
- The appointment request is never opened or is deleted.

If the organization sets a goal that all appointments should be processed and the patient informed of the outcome of the request within 24 hours of the request, the managers will need to know the outcome of each request, the point of delay in the process, if any, and the individual(s) responsible for processing the request. This will require tracking a lot of information around this process that we would recommend building prior to the test phase of your PHR.

All incoming requests will need to have a date/time stamp of when the patient sent the request. Further, there needs to be a date/time stamp and identification of the individual who opens or deletes the request and whether or not an appointment was made, with a date/time stamp associated with that task. Finally, the system needs to track if an outcome message was returned to the patient with the date/time stamp of that action. It is important to note that even in a single organization environment with the organization deploying software supplied by a single vendor for both the scheduling and PHR components, these reports may be extremely difficult to create as the data may exist in disparate databases.

Of the above possible outcome scenarios the only two that are acceptable are:

• The appointment is scheduled as requested and the patient receives a message informing them of the outcome within 24 hours of the request being made by the patient.
• The appointment cannot be scheduled as requested and the patient receives a message informing them of the outcome within 24 hours of the request being made by the patient.

All of the other outcomes would require intervention on the part of the manager to improve the process and thereby enhance the customer experience and use of the PHR. Clearly, the above references one example of the many end user and system performance reports that will be required once your system is implemented. Tracking customer satisfaction, customer features and functions and enhancement requests is also very important to the success of your project. This can readily be achieved by integrating an off-the-shelf (OTS) survey tool with your ePHR.

HEALTHCARE CONSUMER SIGN UP AND ACCESS

There are many models of patient sign up, with different considerations associated with each of them.

In Person

If the consumer is present within the organization, he or she could present with a photo ID to any of the check-in desks throughout the organization to request an ePHR account. The person at the desk could give the requesting consumer an ePHR letter with the information for the consumer's initial log-in to the system. The system would then direct the user to create his or her own private user name and password. The organization might also supply kiosks for this purpose and, though costly, might consider having on-site personnel to be available to assist consumers through the initial log-in.

This scenario involves:

- Training all of the desk personnel regarding signing consumers up for the system.
- Having available an ePHR administrative utility that allows the desk personnel to enter specific information from the patient's valid photo identification to generate an account letter that contains instructions to guide the patient through the account creation process.

This is a costly process that is likely to generate a high number of help desk calls from patients requiring assistance.

Mail

Consumers can also sign up online and be mailed a one-time initial access code to use to sign up online on their own computers. Some organizations have selected this method, as it is a federal crime to open another individual's mail. But this method has decreased in popularity as industry standards have moved to online sign up because mail sign up is more costly and there is an increased likelihood that this process may result in numerous help desk calls. In addition, for a consumer who is used to having instant access to a Web account, it is difficult and frustrating to have to wait several days to receive the mailed letter.

Online Instant Access

This form of sign up access would be available from any Internet browser: from a PC in a waiting area within the organization, to an Internet browser in the patient's home, or anywhere in the world. In general, this process would be similar to how we sign up for most Web sites today, but with heightened security. The healthcare consumer would go to the organization's PHR online sign-up site and enter identifying information. The information entered would be validated against the information that the organization has on file for the healthcare consumer. If all of the information matches, the consumers may then go in and set up their personal log-on ID and password and begin to use the system. If the information does not match after three attempts, consumers would be advised to sign up in person. Prior to allowing access, the organization may want to alert the online user to the fact that falsifying one's identity online to access the system is a crime.

This process is far less costly than above as it generates fewer help desk calls, there is no mailing expense, and it does not require staffing. It also pleases consumers who want immediate access to their account and information.

Clearly, the more independence the consumer will have in signing up for and accessing their account, the lower the costs and the greater the consumer satisfaction.

Some considerations for the help desk in launching a PHR are whether to use your standard tech support help desk. These individuals generally service internal employees; therefore, they will require training and scripts if you are going to have them assist your consumers. Consideration should also be given to anticipating the number of calls and potentially hiring additional help desk support. Alternatively, you may have to create a budget and roll out plan that takes into consideration monitoring the help desk and project staffing needs as the project expands.

User ID and Password

Using industry standards for guiding the consumer in creating a user ID and a "strong" password is recommended. In addition, you should use industry standards for help with a forgotten password and emailing a forgotten user ID/password to the consumer. These should only be emailed to the email address on file provided by the consumer at initial sign up. Any time a forgotten password or user ID is emailed to the consumer, a message regarding that activity should appear in the ePHR.

Logout and Timeout

The rationale and importance of logout and timeout should be covered in any initial materials provided to the consumer or in the site FAQs. A short period of inactivity before timeout due to the sensitive nature of materials on the Web site is recommended.

Terms and Conditions

The project team should draft the site terms and conditions of use document. Once this is drafted, the document should include a bulleted, layperson-friendly summary. The document should be reviewed by your healthcare consumer advisor group for clarity and ability to understand the agreement as well as by your legal counsel.

The document should be posted on the Web site per industry standard with the consumer checking in the "agree with terms and conditions box." However, we recommend that the bulleted summary be fully visible above this check box. It is also recommended that the site clearly state that in no case should the PHR be used for medical urgencies or emergencies. This should be reiterated throughout your collateral materials and on any Web pages that a consumer is sending out communication to your organization. A link should always be available to the "Terms and Conditions" from the PHR and an explanation of them. Finally, a bulleted, layperson-friendly terms and conditions summary should be included in the FAQs (frequently asked questions).

Security

It is recommended that industry standard security measures be implemented, with portal infrastructure using a secure server utilizing 128-bit SSL encryption and a DMZ model. Information should be provided to consumers regarding the ePHR security, with a link on the site to layperson-friendly information about site security. This information should also be available in the FAQs.

Proxy

The purpose of proxy accounts is to facilitate caregivers being able to care for their dependent loved ones. There are many potential caregiver models, including:
• Parents or legal guardian of dependent children;
• Parents or legal guardian of adult disabled children; and
• Child or legal guardian of dependent adult.
State law may vary regarding the rules for legal guardianship and durable power of attorney for healthcare. Your system should be designed to facilitate the flow of needed information exchange for caregivers, while support existing laws.

Site Usability and Development of Site Text

In order to support the needs of all of your constituents, it is recommended that the Web site support the needs of individuals with disabilities (using the National Institute on Disability and Rehabilitation Guidelines for Accessible Web Design or another Web design disability standard), with text written in layperson-friendly, readily comprehensible terms geared at the average reading level. As part of the project change management process described above, creating a consumer advisory council is recommended. The more that you can involve end users in the process, the more buy-in to the project you will create, provided that you listen to their input and incorporate their suggestions into the project. Having created these groups, they should be involved in a review and test of the design as well as a review and critique of the site text.

In addition to the text for the Web pages, you will need to develop the following additional documents:
- Terms and conditions of use
- FAQs
- Instruction guide
- Page-specific site help
- Privacy statement
- Training materials
- Marketing collaterals

All medical terminology or jargon, including all procedure and diagnosis codes International Statistical Classification of Diseases and Related Health Problems (ICD9) and Current Procedural Terminology (CPT) should be translated into layperson-friendly terms and both the original and the "translated" term should be made available to the end user in the ePHR.

Links

The site should include extensive opportunities for searches for layperson-friendly information, as well as information about organizations, individual clinicians, quality and costs. The PHR administrative software will require a link management tool. Be sure to follow existing protocols for linking to other Web sites.

APPENDIX

The following is an ePHR Evaluation Checklist, developed by the HIMSS' Tools of Value ePHR Task Force.

HIMSS Electronic Personal Health Records (ePHR) Checklist[*]

This checklist is provided to assist in the evaluation of an ePHR against HIMSS' established definition and recommended features and functionality. If you have any questions about this checklist, please refer to the HIMSS ePHR Definition in the Appendix in Chapter 3.

---

[*] Used by permission of HIMSS. The authors wish to thank Karen Golden-Russell for this contribution.

ePHR Provider/Vendor

One or more of the following may be checked.

☐	Obtained from patient's healthcare provider(s).
☐	Obtained from patient's employer.
☐	Obtained from patient's health plan.
☐	Obtained from the government.
☐	Obtained from an Internet site.
☐	Obtained from patient's pharmacy.
☐	Obtained from a disease management vendor engaged with the patient.
☐	Obtained from a device manufacturer.

Content Entry

One of the following must be checked.

☐	*Un-tethered/Disconnected* content model: ePHR content is the result of direct entry from the patient or his or her legal proxy(s).
	OR
☐	*Tethered/Connected* content model: An Internet portal that receives data from one organization that participates in the individual's healthcare, such as an institutional EMR/EHR or health insurance claims database. Allows patients or proxies to enter their own data (such as journals and diaries). The institution that provides the ePHR owns and manages the ePHR, allowing patient access.
	OR
☐	*Interoperable* content model: An Internet portal that receives data from multiple constituents that participate in the individual's healthcare, such as pharmacies, hospitals, health insurers, etc. Allows patients or proxies to enter their own data (such as journals and diaries). *Federated:* The ePHR contains pointers to data on the various constituents' databases. *Central database:* Data from various constituents is copied to a central database for viewing within the ePHR.

Security and Access Features

All of the following must be checked to comply with HIMSS' recommendations.

☐	Unique patient identification.
☐	Owned, managed and shared by the individual or his or her legal proxy(s).
☐	Allows secure access to the information contained in the ePHR.
☐	Allows designation of information to be shared electronically with the patient's consent.
☐	Permits the receipt of email alerts that do not reveal protected health information (PHI).
☐	Permits the designation of information to be shared electronically.
☐	Has ability to designate read-only access to the ePHR (or designated portions thereof).
☐	Provides technical support to ePHR constituents at all times.
☐	Allows consumers to export data from their ePHR (portable).
☐	Allows providers, with patient/proxy consent, to export data out of ePHRs or mine data from ePHRs for legitimately defined purposes, such as population health research or health trend analysis.
☐	Provides log of both information shared and information recorded (or entered into the ePHR), including an audit trail of who has entered, accessed, or modified the information.
☐	Provides access to the privacy policy of the source or offerer of the ePHR.

REFERENCES

1. Health Level Seven. What is HL7? Available at www.hl7.org.
2. Miller H. Unpublished study. 2006.
3. Liederman EM, Lee JC, Baquero VH, Seites PG. The impact of patient-physician Web messaging on provider productivity. *JHIM*. 2005; 19(2):81–86.

Chapter 8

PHR Law

The primary ePHR legal concept is that there is no ePHR law, but rather laws that impact the development and use of ePHRs. While political winds swirl around concepts like ownership of healthcare information, a more rational approach with respect to the ePHR would be to examine the nature of the legal relationships necessary for the development and use of one.[1] For legal purposes, the ePHR is an electronic structure populated by information derived from multiple sources for use as directed by the consumer. To the extent that the information is under the control of the consumer, issues of transmission of information are less contentious. The relationships necessary to develop a usable ePHR include those: (1) between the consumer and the ePHR; (2) between the consumer and sources of information about the consumer; and (3) between the consumer and the provider who has access to the information in the ePHR. In this chapter, we will address pertinent legal issues including corporate structure, privacy and security, and liability that will apply to ePHRs. The common denominator in all of these relationships and issues is the consumer. The ePHR is a *personal* health record; it contains information about the subject. Yet, the law does not define the nature of the bundle of relationships that defines the ePHR.

The legal issues we address in this chapter include:
1. Ownership, custody and rights with respect to access and transmission;
2. Privacy and security; and
3. Liability.

OWNERSHIP, CUSTODY AND RIGHT TO DETERMINE ACCESS AND TRANSMISSION OF AN ePHR

The relationship between the ePHR and the consumer depends upon the type of ePHR, how and where it is hosted, and the financial and legal arrangement between the consumer and the developer of the ePHR (hereinafter, the "PHR Supplier"). One of the great circumventions of the public policy debate over HIT policy is ownership of personal health information and health records. The ePHR is the only record of health information that might be owned by the consumer. By ownership, we mean the right to possess, alienate, subdivide or alter the ePHR. Yet, ownership of the ePHR is at once more complicated and less informative than generally understood, as it is for any type of possession, including common items such as homes and automobiles, each of which are subject to myriad restrictions. Indeed, even at best, consumer possession of an ePHR does not include the ability to buy, sell, divide or change the PHR, only under certain circumstances, the information it contains. Even with the PHR, with the exception of self-created ePHRs, the commercially available ePHRs are licensed, rather than sold to the consumer. Even tethered ePHRs, offered to consumers without charge by health plans or providers and pre-populated with PHI, are not so much owned as leased or lent through a licensing agreement. While the PHI may be controlled by the consumer, the consumer's rights to the ePHR as software are strictly prescribed in this manner.

Licensing means that the consumer is paying for a limited set of rights with respect to the software. These include the right to populate it with information, access the product at all times, potentially obtain information through third party links which supply information to consumers through the ePHR, permit others to access the information on it, transmit copies of the PHR and so on. The ePHR may be stored on a personal computer, on portable devices such as thumb drives or CD-ROMs, or hosted on a secure Web site. As we will discuss, the location of storage is a critical determinant with respect to the applicable law.

CONSUMER RIGHTS: RELATIONSHIP TO THE PHR SUPPLIER-LICENSING AGREEMENT

Regardless of the financial relationship between the consumer and the ePHR supplier, the relationship will be marked by specific and commercially common, if not uniform, limitations and restrictions, usually in the form of a license. By common, if not uniform, limitations, we mean that the consumer would be challenged to obtain an ePHR without similar license provisions.

First, the license will uniformly disclaim responsibility for the content of the ePHR and its use. The ePHR supplier appropriately seeks to provide the use of the ePHR, not to be a source of medical advice (though certainly there are cases when the ePHR is tethered to a provider where there are patient physician communications that are meant to be medical advice). In addition to liability concerns, the ePHR supplier is not a physician. Even if the organization is founded, operated, fronted or otherwise headed by a physician, the ePHR supplier is not a physician or licensed entity. Moreover, the consumer and ePHR supplier generally do not have a physician-patient relationship and the interaction does not constitute a medical exam (by practice in all states, by law in others). Having said that, it is possible that providers might develop ePHRs for their patients to use as a tool for communicating medical advice. In that case, the ePHR might be considered part of the delivery of healthcare and liability might attend to the provider as host or supplier as well as to the provider as practitioner.

The license between the ePHR supplier (which may also be the host, like a health plan or provider) and the consumer generally will include the provisions to protect the ePHR supplier from liability to the consumer for use of the information on or available through the ePHR. The liability issues recognize the nature of the substantive information contained in the ePHR: it will derive from a source other than the ePHR supplier, including payors, providers, the consumer, third party vendors and so on. Potential liability derives from the source and use of the information, not from the functioning of the software that hosts the information. The distinction is between the data and the software. The license language also protects the ePHR supplier's intellectual property rights in the software design of the ePHR.

The license will also limit the use of the content, the Web site and affiliated services for personal, not commercial, use. The ePHR is not a vehicle for purposes outside the healthcare of the consumer. Moreover, the consumer is not permitted to invite others into the structure of the ePHR for commercial purposes. The consumer can populate the ePHR and transmit information out, but not permit others to mine the ePHR software, only its data. The consumer controls the flow of information, not the use of ePHR software functions.

The license will describe the incidents of ownership, restrictions on use, copyrights and intellectual property issues. This license provision explains that all rights to the ePHR structure and content, other than PHI, belong to the ePHR supplier. Since the ePHR is effectively a virtual repository, the license distinguishes between ownership of the proprietary technology of the ePHR supplier and the rights of the consumer to his/her health information and the applicable health and wellness information provided by or through the ePHR. Generally, the ePHR supplier's interests are in the software and not the information. By contrast, the consumer's interests are generally in the information and not the software.

Therefore, the license will establish that the rights in the structure—the architecture of the ePHR—remains with the ePHR supplier and that the consumer only receives those rights with respect to the ePHR that are specifically granted. The license will specifically prohibit any action that would or could compromise the intellectual property rights of the ePHR supplier; that is, any action that would expose the software design of any component of the ePHR. Typical language in a licensing agreement would prohibit the copying, disclosure, decompiling, disassembling and creation of derivative works; dissemination; distribution; engineering; reverse engineering; and modifying, renting, sub-licensing or other distribution of the ePHR.

Given the breadth of this language, the key for the consumer includes the limited right to deploy the ePHR for his or her own healthcare; the right to transmit the ePHR to providers for the purpose of informing diagnosis or treatment; and the right to limit the use of ePHR consumer data by the ePHR supplier or anyone else who may receive it. Finally, the license will mandate that no version of the ePHR can be used without the inclusion of relevant indices of the intellectual property rights of the supplier such as trademarks, patents and copyrights.

Naturally, the ePHR supplier will seek to assign responsibility to the consumer for issues beyond the PHR supplier's control. Examples of such issues include the obligation of the consumer to maintain equipment necessary to access and use the ePHR; for maintaining confidentiality of the ePHR including user id and password; and not to populate the ePHR with illegal or inappropriate content. Additionally, once the consumer accesses the ePHR, he/she becomes responsible for its use, not the ePHR supplier. The license will state that the consumer is solely responsible for the consumer data in the ePHR (for example, obtaining legal authority to populate the ePHR with outside information such as files, data, text images or other information transmitted to the ePHR). Increasingly, the hosts of ePHRs, including suppliers, are also mandating that the consumer warrant to the legality of the information itself; that is, the understood privacy of the ePHR should not be cover for illegal activity such as financial records for unlawful enterprises or child pornography.

The ePHR host and supplier through the license appropriately will make the consumer responsible for the mundane but essential components of the ePHR use and security. It is the consumer and not the ePHR vendor who is responsible for maintaining Internet access, computer equipment, software programs and so on. With respect to security, it is the consumer who is responsible for maintaining the confidentiality of the user information such as the user identification and password as well as to immediately notify the supplier or host of unauthorized access, works, viruses or other hazards transmitted through the ePHR. The consumer is also responsible for updating his or her email address to continue to receive alerts regarding new information that is available in the ePHR, when such a service is offered.

Other license components may include:

- **Limitation of Liability/Disclaimer of Warranties.** This provision will disclaim any responsibility for any content on the PHR site or linked to the ePHR site for use by the consumer. It specifically will disclaim responsibility for accuracy of content or PHI. The limitation on liability will provide the consumer with advance notice of the matters for which the ePHR supplier will take responsibility and for how much. Essentially, these provisions mean that the consumer uses the ePHR at his or her own risk. This or a similar provision will also detail the consumer's responsibilities for security.

- **Privacy Policy.** The idea of a privacy policy derives from the HIPAA privacy regulations which mandate that covered entities have a Notice of Privacy Practices.[2] That requirement, however, does not apply to ePHR suppliers that are not covered entities. To the extent that a consumer obtains an ePHR from an ePHR supplier directly or through an employer or other non-covered entity, HIPAA does not directly apply. Most covered entities that provide ePHRs mandate that their ePHR suppliers have privacy policies that are at least as stringent as their own (i.e., in a tethered environment, HIPAA protections would apply if the host of the ePHR would be a covered entity and the ePHR supplier will assume the responsibilities of a business associate). Moreover, as a matter of marketing, ePHR suppliers are often compelled to provide HIPAA-like protections and describe these protections in their privacy policies. The consumer's rights, however, are defined by the license and cannot rely upon best practices, especially if the application of HIPAA or state laws are unclear with respect to the ePHR. The consumer's rights are exercised through consideration of the ePHR license that addresses HIPAA and state law issues.

CONSUMER RIGHTS IN ePHR – DETERMINATION OF ACCESS AND CONTENT

Once the edifice of the ePHR is obtained (i.e., licensed from the ePHR supplier), we can address the consumer's rights in the ePHR. First, the right of transmission and access is both defined by the license and by law. The consumer can grant access to anyone through use of the passwords and other security measures. Likewise, no law prohibits a consumer from sharing content available through the ePHR for treatment or care purposes; this content is available for the consumer to use, but not to retransmit the entire PHR for commercial purposes.

PRIVACY AND SECURITY

Ultimately, the legal import of ownership is subsumed by the ability to determine the content and transmission of the ePHR as an instrument. The primary applicable federal law is HIPAA[3] and the implementing regulations known as the Privacy and Security Rules.[4]

Essentially, the HIPAA Privacy and Security Rules directly apply to covered entities such as (1) health plans; (2) healthcare clearinghouses; or (3) healthcare providers that transmit any health information in electronic form in connection with standard transactions. The rules apply indirectly to "business associates, those entities which assist covered entities in performing treatment payment or operations functions." HIPAA mandates that covered entities have business associate agreements with the business associate that contractually assure that the business associate will comply with those components of HIPAA applicable to the function being provided.

HIPAA impacts the ePHR relationships in a number of ways. If the ePHR is hosted by a covered entity, then the HIPAA rules apply to the host as host and it has independent obligations under HIPAA. HIPAA does not directly regulate the ePHR hosts and the ePHR vendors that are not covered entities. Therefore, commercial hosts of PHRs, such as HealthVault and Google, are not directly covered by HIPAA. While the host and vendor may assume certain limited HIPAA obligations through the license, they generally do not assume to provide the full range of HIPAA protections nor should they.

HIPAA's greatest impact on ePHRs is in the population of the ePHR with PHI. A covered entity may use or disclose PHI as follows:
- For the treatment, payment or healthcare operations of a covered entity.
- For the treatment activities of a healthcare provider .
- To a covered entity or a healthcare provider for the payment activities of the recipient.
- To a covered entity for healthcare operations activities of the recipient, if each entity either has or had a relationship with the individual who is the subject of the PHI being requested, the PHI pertains to such relationship, and the disclosure is:
    - For a purpose defined as healthcare operations; or
    - For the purpose of healthcare fraud and abuse detection or compliance.
- Note that the right of an individual consumer to receive his or her PHI under HIPAA obviates the need for a covered entity to receive specific authorization for every transmission of that person's PHI to an ePHR. Having said that, for security purposes, the ePHR hosts will want some form of authentication and authorization prior to accepting information from any party other than the consumer.
- All authorizations under HIPAA must contain an expiration date; patients must be advised of their right to revoke the authorization at any time; and the authorization must be written in plain language. So the use of authorizations will require a significant amount of additional bookkeeping, legal and clerical time in order to assure compliance with the detailed regulatory provisions, though the process can be automated.

There is another important consideration that must be dealt with regarding uses and disclosures of PHI—the "minimum necessary" rule.[5] The general rule is that when using or disclosing PHI or when requesting PHI from another covered entity, a covered entity must make reasonable efforts to limit PHI to the minimum necessary to accomplish the intended purpose of the use, disclosure or request. For ePHR purposes, the minimum necessary rule does not apply to (among other things) uses/disclosures made to the individual or made pursuant to an authorization. Having said that, HIPAA and state laws limit or prohibit the transmission of certain types of information in the absence of and sometimes even with the authorization of the consumer. Behavioral health records, genetic information and HIV/AIDS information are types of information, depending upon the state, that may be subject to special rules regarding authorization for transmission of PHI. While this does not apply to transmission of information by the consumer from the consumer's ePHR, it does apply to the manner in which such information may be transmitted to the ePHR from a provider of such services.

Those covered entities that contribute data to or obtain data from an ePHR must comply with the Privacy and Security Rules and, to the greatest extent possible, ensure that the ePHR host or vendor complies as well. For the covered entity, transmission of PHI to and receipt of PHI from an ePHR creates legal risk. Inappropriate transmission to an ePHR would be a HIPAA violation (unless authorized by the consumer). Acceptance of PHI from an ePHR creates liabilities with respect to the quality and integrity of the ePHR Data.

PHR SECURITY

Responsibility for the security of the PHR is shared among the PHR supplier, host and consumer. HIPAA mandates a security officer for covered entities and the responsibilities would likely extend to a tethered ePHR. For non-tethered ePHRs, the host, supplier and consumer would engage in a division of functions. The consumer is responsible for the security of identification and passwords. The host is responsible for the risk analysis of the likelihood and criticality of threats to the security of the ePHR. The host is also responsible for authenticating the identity and authorization for contributors to and recipients of ePHR data. As important, the host needs to assure that unauthorized persons do not receive ePHR data to prevent inappropriate disclosures. The supplier, in designing the architecture, must also account for patient identification, authentication and data exchange. Ultimately, among the three parties, security safeguards should be implemented to support the permitted uses and disclosures and to prevent forbidden uses and disclosures.

THE CURIOUS PARANOIA ABOUT EMPLOYER AND HEALTH PLAN ACCESS

A spurious objection to electronically stored PHI is that employers and insurers will have access to it and will abuse that access. The penalties for such abuse are grave and far exceed any potential benefit to an organization that might seek such information.[6] It is important to note that in addition to HIPAA and the Employment Retirement Income Security Act (ERISA), it is likely that ePHRs will be subject to the Stored Communications Act that prohibits obtaining electronic communications by intentional access without authorization.[7] It also prohibits the release of information by the operator of a "remote computing service" from releasing information to any private party without the "lawful consent" of the subscriber. While the Stored Communications Act is not so explicit, the term "remote computing service" could be reasonably interpreted to include an ePHR not otherwise covered by HIPAA (i.e., one not tethered to a covered entity). Under ERISA, the administrator would be subject to sanction as well for inappropriate disclosure of information to the sponsor, creating a third party with liability for misused information. So, the law with respect to protecting consumer information is more than adequate. Short of prohibiting the use of digital information technology for PHI, diligent enforcement should be an adequate remedy for consumers.

It is important to recognize that the absence of a complete and unique law of personal health records does not mean that there are either no standards in law or a complete and unique approach under other guises. For example, a private sector collaborative of over 100 organizations, led by the Markle Foundation, developed an outline for the regulation of the creations, storage and exchange of health information, known as the "Common Framework for Networked Personal Health Information" (see www.connectingforhealth.org). The Common Framework establishes nine consumer policies and seven technology parameters that would govern the storage and exchange of PHI. While the Common Framework is not law, it is effectively an accreditation standard, albeit one not yet adopted by any payor or deemed as satisfying legal requirements by any regulatory body.

ePHRs AND LEGAL MEDICAL RECORDS

Merely because PHI is input into an ePHR does not grant that information special status wherever else it might exist. The information in an ePHR is likely to be a composite of data from payors, providers, pharmacies and laboratories, each of which is legally mandated to maintain clinical and claims information. While the consumer controls the PHI in the ePHR, the consumer has more circumscribed rights with respect to medical records held by others for their own purposes. For example, physicians are required by licensure regulations to maintain medical records for each of their patients that "accurately, legibly and completely reflect the evaluation and treatment of the patient." The medical records must identify the patient; contain dated entries signed by the physician; reflect the patient's complaints and symptoms; include the physician's diagnosis, findings and results of pathologic, clinical laboratory or radiology examination; reference medical and surgical treatment; outline other diagnostic, corrective or therapeutic procedures; list prescriptions and over-the-counter drugs; and highlight recommended inpatient and outpatient treatments. Physicians must maintain these records for a specified period (in Pennsylvania, for example, that time period is the greater of one year past the age of majority or seven years).[8]

Physicians and other covered entities also have the duty to provide the record to their patients upon request, unless the physicians believe the release of the information would adversely affect the patient's health.[9] Further, they must appropriately complete forms and maintain records necessary for reimbursement by a patient's health plan. It should be noted that only one state, New Hampshire, recognizes medical records as the property of the patient and, even then, the property right only entitles the patient to a copy of the record at a reasonable cost.[10]

In addition to physicians, other practitioners and facilities have similar obligations, but records would also include admission and discharge notes as well as pre-and post-surgical notes.[11]

The ePHR differs from provider medical records in that there are no content, continuity or maintenance requirements. There are no penalties for failure to maintain an ePHR. By contrast, failure to appropriately maintain medical records could subject a provider or payor to licensure, accreditation and certification—and in some states even criminal—sanctions.

LIABILITY AND INDEMNIFICATION[12]

ePHR suppliers and covered entities face three types of liability related to the use of health information: breach of privacy obligations; professional/medical malpractice liability for failure or misuse of information; and professional/medical malpractice liability for transmission of inaccurate information.

Breach of privacy obligations may arise from case law or from specific statutory recognition of the cause of action. While the HIPAA enforcement mechanism is overseen by HHS and the U.S. Justice Department, many state laws specifically provide for private enforcement action as well as state action for security breaches. Moreover, some state attorney generals have found security enforcement to be a platform issue. Note the importance of assumption of liability in the licensing agreement. To the extent that there are privacy or security breaches, the relationship between the ePHR supplier and the consumer—as well as the relationship between the ePHR supplier and the covered entity—involve the delegation of responsibility for the transmission of healthcare information inappropriately, for breaches of security and for the integrity of the content provided. Because provision of data to a consumer is mandated by law, and the ePHR is merely the vehicle for storage and transmission of the ePHR, these concerns cannot derail ePHR development. There is simply no basis on which a covered entity can outright refuse to make information available to a consumer who requests it.

By contrast, the law of medical malpractice liability is very well developed. The questions raised by the use of healthcare information transmitted in an ePHR environment include: who bears the liability for the content of the information exchanged; whether the consolidation of information into a common form creates potential for medical malpractice or another form of liability (impacting the use of experts and, depending upon the state, the amount of recovery); and whether the existence of an available source of information specific to a patient creates an obligation on the part of the provider to consult that source of information.

By way of short background, the elements of any medical malpractice case are few: there must be an injury or adverse event; the standard of care, established by expert testimony, must have been breached; and the breach must be the proximate cause of the injury.

Therefore, placing ePHR in the medical malpractice context, the question is how the standard of care will be interpreted and applied. Will the standard of care ultimately include responsibility on the part of each contributor to validate the information transmitted to or received from the ePHR? Will the standard establish the responsibility of a treating provider to obtain available sources of information including a PHR? Will the standard establish the responsibility of parties such as payors to provide information to the ePHR?

The standard of care with respect to healthcare provider use of available information is evolving. Courts have provided mixed decisions: the court in Primus v. Galliano indicates that physicians must consult available records.[13] In Suniga v. Eyre and Susnis v. Radfar, the courts held no such obligation exists.[14] Interestingly, courts have given judicial recognition to the obligation, if not rendering a decision on that point.[15] To the extent that the entire development of American liability law recognizes that adoption of innovations leads to developments of higher expectations and therefore higher standards of care, we can expect that the increased availability of healthcare information in an inexpensive and useful format will lead to a standard of care that establishes the responsibility of the provider to use such information. Innovation leads to higher standards—for example, witness fetal monitoring, glaucoma testing and nurse call center cases.[16]

ePHR suppliers and hosts also need to be concerned that the developing standards include responsibilities for the accuracy of information in the ePHR. As previously discussed, the responsibility for some of the potential liability will be negotiated as part of the license between the consumer and the ePHR supplier and perhaps the host. It is premature to assign actual liability in advance. There exist too many variables. Is the data accurate, inaccurate, subject to interpretation? Was sufficient data available to lead inexorably to one conclusion rather than another? Has the consumer altered the data? What is the impact of consumer alterations to PHI contributed by providers? Whose version of events/diagnoses prevails? What is the impact of practice enhancements on health professional liability or on the payors that P4P?

Inevitably, these issues will be resolved in the legal cauldron of experience and alleged misfortune. Consistent with the lessons of Helling v. Carey, however, the deliberate inclusion of inaccurate information in a PHR by a covered entity, or the deliberate ignorance of information contained in a readily accessible PHR, are likely to result in the assignment of liability on the covered entity which fails to act in a manner that the courts believe will be consistent with an appropriate standard of care.

Some physician advocates have noted that the potential use of ePHRs, like the increased use of Internet research by consumers, will increase the work for physicians because they will be obliged to review an additional document. As we observe elsewhere in this book, the increased workload and uncertainty of the source of the data may be considered barriers to physician acceptance. Worse, they will not be reimbursed for this additional mandatory effort. Observe, initially, that there is no case law that indicates that a physician's duty to review a patient's medical record is limited by reimbursement. True, there is no law which indicates that a physician must review an ePHR, but the standard is likely to be established based upon the ease of obtaining the information. The more accessible the relevant information, the greater likelihood that a court will determine that the standard is to review the information. So, a well organized ePHR with readily accessible information is more likely to mitigate toward review. Several hundred pages of claims information, by contrast, will not. Back again to Helling v. Carey and Das v. Thani, the key to a paradigm shift in the standard of care is the change in the standard. The standard will change when the technology makes it so easy that it cannot reasonably be ignored. At that time, it is also likely that the time involved in reviewing an ePHR will be substantially shorter or the question mitigated by the fact that the ePHR data will flow seamlessly into the physician's EMR tagged with its origin.

Finally, the unique nature of the ePHR and the consumer's role in populating and editing the content will create skepticism on the part of providers. As the use of electronic health information evolves, similar to what occurred with like growth of the Internet, we will get both useful and useless information; valid and invalid results. While no law currently exists with respect to limitations on liability or indemnification for use of consumer provided information, such law will develop over time.

REFERENCES

1. By ePHR, we refer only to electronic PHRs that store digitized information.
2. 45 C.F.R. §164.520.
3. Pub. L. No. 104-191.
4. 45 C.F.R. Secs 160, 162 and 164.
5. § 164.502(b).
6. The Employee Retirement Income Security Act of 1974 ("ERISA") (Pub. L. 94-406, 88 Stat. 829, September 2, 1974.
7. 18 U.S.C. Sec. 2701 et. Seq.
8. e.g., in Pennsylvania, 49 Pa.Code §16.95.
9. e.g., in HIPAA, 45 C.F.R. §164.524(a); and by way of example, in Pennsylvania, 49 Pa.Code §16.61.
10. N.H. Rev. Stat. Ann. §151:21 (2006). See Waller A. Getting information rights right. Available at: http://library.ahima.org/xpedio/groups/public/documents/ahima/bok1_032269.hcsp?dDoc. Accessed June 12, 2008.
11. Pennsylvania Hospital License regulations, 28 Pa.Code §115.31.
12. Burde HA, Fox SJ, Szabo DS. *RHIOs and HIPAA.* In Thielst CB, Jones LE, eds. *Guide to Establishing a Regional Health Information Organization.* Chicago: HIMSS; 2007.
13. 329 F.3d 236 (1st Cir. 2003).
14. Suniga v. Eyre, 2004 Tex. App. LEXIS 486 (4th Dis. 2004). Susnis v. Radfar, 317 Ill. App. 3d 817 (1st Dist. 5th Div. 2000).
15. e.g., Chapa v United States, 2006 U.S. Dist. Lexis 42757 at item 52; and Hedger v. Reliance Standard Life Insurance Company, 2005 U.S. Dist. Lexis 37071.
16. Das. V. Thani, 171 N.J. 518, (N.J. Sup. Ct. 2002), Helling v. Carey, 83 Wn. 2d 514, (Wash. 1974), Shannon v. McNulty, 718 A.2d 828 (Pa. Super. Ct. 1998).

CHAPTER 9

PHR Business Sustainability Models

DEFINITION AND IMPORTANCE OF BUSINESS SUSTAINABILITY

A business or other organization may be considered sustainable when its ongoing revenues are predictably and consistently equal to or greater than its expenses. Clearly, a new business must rapidly achieve such sustainability to survive. Therefore, in developing a business plan for any new business, an essential component is the financial plan that will ultimately lead to net positive revenue. Otherwise, the considerable time, effort, and investment involved in starting the business may be futile. More to the point, investors, customers and business partners are likely to demand some form of assurance or at least reasoned analysis to satisfy their needs.

Implicit in the concept of sustainability is the notion that a new business initially has a "startup" phase where expenses exceed revenue as investments are made to build the organization, products, and services that comprise the business. Since few businesses are able to generate any revenue before offering products and services to customers, a typical startup phase only has expenses while revenue is zero. Once revenues begin, they typically do not immediately cover all the expenses. A business "breaks even" when revenue increases to the point that is equal to expenses.

So sustainability applies to the situation after "startup" when revenues at least cover expenses. The impact of startup costs on sustainability depends in part on the type of organization. In a "for-profit" organization, initial investors typically receive "equity" in the form of shares of ownership in the company. If the organization is consistently profitable, its overall value (and the value of the shares held by investors) increases, validating the investments.

In non-profit organizations, the impact of startup costs relates to the source of funding. If the funding was "contributed" through grants or gifts, then there is no impact. However, if loans were provided, then the ongoing expenses include whatever repayments are required under the loan terms.

The anticipated sustainability of a functioning business does not in itself guarantee that there is a feasible path to achieving it. Even though it may be possible to describe a "steady state" business that delivers needed services at an affordable price to customers who are anxious to pay for it, there may be insurmountable obstacles to creating such a business. A clear example of this issue is Federal Express. Prior to establishing FedEx, it was possible to describe a sustainable business that delivered packages overnight for a large number of customers at a reasonable price. However, it was a huge challenge to attract sufficient investment to build the initial infrastructure to provide limited service, followed by additional investment to expand the infrastructure rapidly to increase the customer base to achieve sustainability. Large, risky startup costs such as those that were needed for FedEx can prove to be an insurmountable challenge.

ELEMENTS OF BUSINESS SUSTAINABILITY

Two basic elements contribute to business sustainability: cost and revenue. Since prospects for business sustainability improve with either lower costs or increased revenue, keeping costs low through efficient system and organizational design and processes is essential.

For an ePHR, this means maximizing the use of automated processes that do not require continuing personnel support.

There are a wide range of potential revenue sources for ePHR systems: (1) subscription fees; (2) sponsorship; (3) advertising; (4) secondary use of data; (5) value-added services; and (6) reduced healthcare costs. Subscription fees refer to periodic payments made by users of ePHR systems (typically by consumers). Some ePHR systems that depend on other sources of revenue may waive such fees, offering "free" services.

Sponsorship includes payments from third parties who benefit from the ePHR, such as physician groups, health insurers or employers. Typically, the perceived benefit to the sponsor involves providing enhanced service to their customers as well as encouraging brand loyalty. However, when the latter is the goal, it is often difficult to enlist the cooperation of other competing organizations in the provision of data. This tends to limit the ePHR to data provided solely by the sponsor, thereby reducing its value since it is not (and cannot be) complete.

Advertising has been a very successful revenue source for many Internet providers of information services. Google, for example, has become extremely successful by providing high quality search capabilities at no charge while reaping substantial revenue from advertisers who pay for a share of the attention of the users. Clearly, there is similar potential for advertising revenue from carefully selected promotional material presented in the context of consumer use of their ePHR. Microsoft recently announced HealthVault™,[1] a search and storage site for ePHRs that is expected to generate most of its operational revenue in this way. It is not clear at this time how much advertising revenue can be expected from ePHR sites, and whether it can be sufficient to fund a substantial fraction of the cost of an ePHR system. It is also unclear how, if at all, HealthVault, Google and other third party repositories will assess the integrity and validity of the advertisers' products and services. Of course, medical advertising within ePHRs must be done in an ethical and appropriate manner, subject to the same consumer protections and FDA oversight as is currently applied in other media.

Secondary use of ePHR data is often cited as a major potential revenue source. Certainly, there is a large existing market for secondary use of health data by insurers, pharmaceutical firms and medical researchers ($billions/year). However, generating such revenue from ePHRs is limited by completeness of the information, size and coverage of the subscriber base, and privacy issues. Ethically, it would be important to ensure that third party servers storing individuals' PHI that use the de-identified information for secondary purposes allow these individuals the opportunity to provide consent for such usage. As ePHRs grow in importance, revenue from secondary use may become more important. At present, however, it is mostly a theoretical possibility that may even have a negative impact on adoption because of consumer privacy concerns.

Value-added services may be a substantial source of income for ePHR systems in the future, particularly as the records become more complete. With all of a person's medical records in one place, it is possible to provide a wide variety of new services that enhance health, convenience, and peace of mind. For health improvement, customized reminders of various types could be generated, such as for needed preventive services (e.g., colonoscopy). Convenience could be enhanced by provision of basic demographic data from the PHR to physicians, thereby eliminating the need for the consumer to repeatedly provide this information manually at each visit on the much-derided "clipboard." An example of a service that could improve "peace of mind" would be immediate electronic notification to children of elderly parents living remotely (e.g., via instant message) when the ePHR of their loved one was accessed by an emergency physician (thereby indicating that their loved one was in an emergency room). Through services such as these, consumers could have greatly enhanced opportunities to more easily maintain and monitor their health.

Reduced healthcare costs represent one of the ultimate expected benefits from ePHRs. The benefit of such reductions in cost would accrue primarily to employers, with lesser (but important) allocations to consumers. Realizing these benefits would increase the ability of employers to provide ePHR sponsorship. For consumers, it would make it easier to pay subscription fees.

It is important to note that widespread use of ePHRs by consumers (and their healthcare providers) will not only require effective, easy-to-use, financially sustainable systems, but also significant changes in behavior. Therefore, any ePHR business model must account for the need to encourage such changes to assure widespread adoption.

FACTORS AFFECTING PHR COSTS

One key factor that has a major impact on ePHR costs is the architecture of the system. As discussed in Chapter 6, a distributed architecture that requires data to be retrieved in real time via queries to multiple independent systems will be very complex (i.e., expensive) to operate. In contrast, the simple architecture of a repository that stores each person's complete records and makes them readily available for rapid retrieval at any time will be much more economical. These differences will apply in both the startup and operational phases of the ePHR; the distributed architecture would be much more costly to implement as well as operate.

Regardless of the architecture, another important cost consideration is the impact of the growth of the subscriber base. The ePHR system infrastructure must be fully in place and operational prior to its use by the first customer, while the incremental cost of adding additional users is very small. Therefore, the costs of creating, and most of the expenses involved in operating this infrastructure are "fixed." The practical implication is that the per-subscriber cost starts very high and then decreases rapidly, much as it does for any business with a complex and expensive fixed infrastructure (such as a phone company or an Internet service provider). This means that there is a "ramp up" phase while the subscriber base grows during which time the business will not be able to cover its expenses, equivalent to the "start up phase" described above. The longer it takes to reach "breakeven," the more investment is required to cover the startup expenses. Therefore, to avoid having those losses accumulate excessively, ePHR suppliers will need to focus on rapidly attaining a sufficiently large number of customers to cover their costs. In this manner, the effectiveness of marketing efforts will be closely linked to financial sustainability.

POTENTIAL SOURCES OF REVENUE

In this section, potential revenue sources of ePHR systems are examined in more detail. Earlier, several types of revenue were described; here specific applications for various stakeholder groups are highlighted.

Healthcare Providers

Besides consumers, the most obvious (and perhaps important) ePHR stakeholder category is healthcare providers, including physicians, hospitals, clinical laboratories and imaging centers. They would benefit from immediate availability of reliable, accurate and complete patient information. At present, providers each have a subset of this information that consists primarily of their own records, in either a paper or electronic format. Since most patients receive their care from multiple providers, each has an incomplete picture. Furthermore, giving providers access to insurance claims data for their patients could be very helpful. For example, only claims data allows a determination of what medication prescriptions have been filled; the providers only know what was prescribed unless they have access to the claims data. Clearly, this latter information would be invaluable in point-of-care prescribing decisions and in evaluating patient compliance with recommended medication regimens.

Despite these benefits, healthcare providers are reluctant to pay for such information. First, the provision of "outside records" has traditionally been free to providers; they do not usually impose fees on each other. In any case, such charges would tend to offset each other since most providers both send and request records from others. As previously discussed, while the availability of fully interoperable records that would automatically and seamlessly update a physician's local EMR would actually be a benefit rather than a burden, the tradition of outside records being "free" would still mitigate against physician payment.

In addition, the benefits of complete information accrue primarily to others in the healthcare system. One study estimated that physicians capture only 11 percent of the benefits of EMRs in their offices, with the balance going to those who pay for care.[2] In addition, quality and safety improvements from complete information have the tendency to decrease revenue when reimbursement is based on a fee-for-service model. For example, if an outpatient has an adverse drug reaction, the most likely outcome is another visit to their physician—which means additional reimbursement. Of course, this is not meant to imply that providers are opposed to increasing quality and safety. However, from a practical standpoint, providers are not likely to welcome requests to pay for technology that will decrease their income. Such a proposition simply does not make economic sense.

Payors

Other important stakeholder groups are payors, including health insurers, health plans, self-insured employers, third party administrators and pharmacy benefit managers (PBMs). The benefits of ePHRs for these organizations include more accurate diagnoses and treatment; reduction of duplicative encounters, diagnostic tests and prescriptions; more rapid and lower cost access to information needed to process claims; and availability of updated information for disease management programs. For example, complete ePHR data could potentially eliminate the need for "claims attachments" since that information would be accessible from the ePHR. Also, disease management programs currently expend significant resources collecting and updating the clinical information necessary to help consumers and providers more effectively address chronic conditions. Therefore, ePHRs potentially offer significant administrative efficiencies to payors.

However, savings from such efficiencies are not proven and their magnitude is not easy to estimate. Moreover, the transition to ePHRs could create inefficiencies as the new processes are introduced at the same time as the old methods must be maintained for those consumers who do not yet have ePHRs. Therefore, capturing the savings, particularly early in the process, may be problematic. Having said that, payors are rapidly creating ePHRs for their members and CMS has launched a pilot project to develop ePHRs for their beneficiaries.

It is noteworthy that the two major associations of health insurers (Blue Cross & Blue Shield Association and America's Health Insurance Plans) have agreed on a minimum data set for ePHRs, and have also agreed that information in an ePHR will be transferred from carrier to carrier when a consumer's coverage changes.[3] However, ePHRs sponsored by payors are not likely to be complete as the other healthcare stakeholders have little incentive to send any information beyond what is needed for claims to them and also are not likely to be trusted by consumers since the information is not under their control. Indeed, 59 percent of healthcare consumers do not trust their health insurer.[4] As a result, it would seem that the efforts by payors to directly provide ePHRs to their beneficiaries actually diminishes the ability of either the organization or the consumer to benefit from them.

Finally, while payors have some interest in lowering healthcare costs to be able to provide a more affordable product to their customers (the employers), they do not directly suffer financially from increasing medical costs (except to the extent that such costs exceed premiums in a given year). As long as employers are willing to fund the premiums needed to cover the healthcare benefits, the payors can prosper financially. The primary motivation for payors to improve care and reduce costs (including administrative costs) comes from pressure exerted by employers.

Employers

Employers clearly have much to gain from the widespread use of ePHRs. Employers fund the bulk of healthcare costs, and are increasingly losing their competitive edge (particularly when competing globally) because of the rapid escalation of health-related expenditures.

As previously discussed in Chapter 4, there is a growing body of evidence that employers that offer ePHRs—along with consumer health and chronic disease management related incentive/disincentive programs—are reaping their financial benefits. To the extent that the availability of ePHRs can reduce costs, employers will be direct and immediate beneficiaries.

A number of employers have realized this and organized efforts to provide ePHRs to their employees. For example, IBM began offering ePHRs to their employees in 2007.[5] As previously mentioned, a consortium of large employers, including Intel® and Wal-Mart®, are collaborating to create Dossia®, a shared system of ePHRs for all their employees.[6] Such efforts require substantial expenditures that are justified based on anticipated savings.

However, employer-based ePHRs suffer from similar drawbacks as those sponsored by payors. Employees are leery of an ePHR controlled directly or indirectly by their employer. There is substantial (and legitimate) concern about the employer accessing this information and using it to discriminate against the employee (with actions up to and including involuntary dismissal). Consumers also are not guaranteed ongoing use of their information should they change jobs. Finally, healthcare providers have little incentive to incur the added costs of providing information to employer-sponsored ePHRs.

Nevertheless, these early efforts by employers do recognize the value of ePHRs. Therefore, sponsorship of independent ePHRs via funding from employers seems to be a reasonable expectation. As long as the employer has no direct connection with or control over the ePHR vendor or access to the ePHR (which in any case is prohibited by law), employee trust should be possible to achieve. Such independent ePHRs would allow the employee to maintain a lifetime ePHR while moving from one employer to another.

Consumers

Consumers are the ultimate (and perhaps greatest) beneficiaries of ePHRs. Today, consumers do not have access to their complete medical records nor are they in a position to enable such access by their healthcare providers. The result of having more complete records available will be higher quality care, fewer medical errors and reduced costs. All three of these benefits accrue directly to consumers, although the advantages of reduced costs are shared with employers (for consumers with health insurance).

Indeed, consumers have already recognized the advantages of more complete records. Even today, many consumers with chronic conditions carry their own medical records from provider to provider. In a 2005 national survey, 52 percent of consumers indicated they would be willing to pay $5 per month or more to have their records in electronic form. A follow-up survey in 2007 found that 51 percent of consumers are willing to pay a "reasonable fee" for this service.[7,8]

Despite this data, the "uptake" of free ePHRs has been very low. While this may initially seem to contradict the surveys, a closer examination helps clarify the issues. Most available "free" ePHRs either require the consumer to manually enter and maintain all the information or only support automatic loading of information from the sponsoring organization (a single provider, fiscal intermediary or employer). Therefore, the information is not likely to be complete. Even if an industrious and compulsive consumer maintains accurate records on his or her own, such information is not likely to be trusted by providers, who will legitimately worry about transcription errors of critical information (such as laboratory tests).

This analysis is further supported by the more substantial use of ePHRs reported by organizations such as Kaiser Permanente. Their tethered ePHR, while not complete, contains most of the information for a given patient since most of their care is obtained at Kaiser. This, combined with the ability to have secure communication with their provider, has resulted in greater adoption of the ePHR system they sponsor. In late 2007, the usage rate of their ePHR by consumers was reported to be 18.4 percent.[9] It is important to note that consumers can receive benefit from these systems even if they do not access them (if an ePHR has comprehensive medical record information from multiple providers that can be used at each encounter to improve care), so consumer usage rates alone are not necessarily indicative of how consumers perceive the value of such systems in their overall healthcare.

Looking at the totality of information with respect to consumer demand and willingness to pay, it appears that consumers are likely to be an important source of revenue for ePHRs if those systems provide real value via complete information entered automatically and directly from trusted sources.

CURRENT BUSINESS MODELS

At the present time, ePHR suppliers appear to be using one or more of three different business models: (1) subscription; (2) sponsorship; and (3) advertising. Although each model may have some variations, it is notable that most of the current vendors appear to depend primarily on a single one of these for the bulk of their revenue.

Subscription Model

The subscription model involves each consumer paying a periodic small fee to the ePHR supplier. One example of this is mymedicalrecords.com, which provides an ePHR with consumer-entered information in the form of scanned-in documents for a standard fee of $9.95/month (that includes online storage of records for up to ten family members). With this model, the consumer typically is given control over the records that are not sold or otherwise made available to third parties. Often employers pay the standard fee for employees.

Sponsorship Model

The sponsorship model can be subdivided into two types: direct sponsorship and secondary use. In the direct sponsorship approach, a healthcare stakeholder (e.g., providers, payors, and employers) provides a free ePHR to its customers, typically as a way to improve brand loyalty. A provider example of this model is Kaiser PHR cited above; a payor example is the Aetna ePHR, provided to all Aetna subscribers. The information in the Aetna ePHR is limited to the claims information received by Aetna, including all the member's provider encounters. Also, as you would expect, other organizations are not inclined to provide additional information to such an ePHR as there is no particular benefit to them for doing so (or, even worse, they may be direct competitors).

In the secondary use variation of the sponsor fee model, the ePHR supplier provides free online records to consumers while generating revenue by aggregating information for sale to third parties. One example of this is zebrahealth.com; in its privacy policy, the company states that it "reserves the right to release aggregate information to third parties," although it claims that this information will not be identifiable. This model also does not provide consumer control of the de-identified information (in aggregate form).

Another variation of the sponsor fee model is medem.com, a non-profit organization sponsored by a consortium including a number of national medical societies. They provide the iHealthRecord™ ePHR that physicians (and other medical organizations) can offer at no charge to their patients. Payments for the service come from physician and hospital group licenses, transaction fees for online physician consultations, integration fees from software companies and customized software fees from health plans and medical manufacturers. There is no advertising. Currently, most of the information in the iHealthRecord is entered by patients, although efforts are underway to allow direct electronic loading of medications and laboratory data. Interfaces are also being built to EMR systems.

Advertising Model

Finally, there is the advertising model, exemplified by Microsoft HealthVault™.[1] Many successful Web sites are currently supported by revenue from advertisers who will pay varying rates for consumer "views" and substantially higher rates when consumers "click-through" to specifically receive additional information about available products or services. Google is perhaps the best example of this business model, having used it successfully to become a multibillion-dollar business. In its most basic form, it depends on generating a large amount of Web site usage since the fees paid by advertisers for each consumer "view" are quite small.

In the context of ePHRs, it is possible for advertising to be customized based on the information in the consumer's ePHR. For example, a consumer who has diabetes could be shown ads for glucose meters. Such "targeted" advertising usually produces a higher response rate and is therefore more valuable to sponsors. The usual and legal incentive is to obtain consumer authorization for such advertising.

In the case of HealthVault, there is an associated search engine customized for health-related searches. When search terms are entered, ads are generated based on those terms. Advertising revenue from the ad sponsors provides the revenue needed for ongoing operations.

VALUE PROPOSITIONS

ePHR systems provide clear value for all the healthcare stakeholders, but the specific value proposition varies. For healthcare providers, the primary benefit would be readily available, complete electronic records for each patient, including information about visits to other providers and institutions (integrated into local EMR systems, if they are in use). Such information is extremely valuable, both in terms of providing better care (e.g., by knowing all the prescriptions that have been filled) and saving time (by avoiding redundant questioning of the patient and/or multiple requests for outside records). The efficiencies from having a single source of complete information are substantial, especially when practitioners consider the extensive staff work that is currently devoted to sending and receiving records. This can be extremely significant in the context of institutions not being reimbursed for iatrogenic conditions, as the provider will want to document all pre-existing conditions prior to admission and also may want to be aware if a patient has particular risks.

However, there also are costs for healthcare providers, particularly for their own EMR systems. In order for an ePHR system to have complete electronic records, each healthcare provider would need to have an EMR that can produce such records for transmittal to the ePHR (integrated into local EMR systems, if they are in use). Cost estimates for acquiring such systems range up to $40,000 per physician, with continuing costs for operation. Furthermore, most of the benefits of EMR systems in physician offices accrue to other healthcare stakeholders.[2] Besides the direct economic costs, the lost productivity during the transition to an EMR as well as the potential for slightly increased record-keeping workloads are obstacles to widespread EMR adoption. Nevertheless, an ePHR system provides clear benefits to healthcare providers regardless of whether or not they have an EMR. The issue is that creating the ePHR system requires that the vast majority of providers have EMRs to supply the electronic information in the first place.

There is ongoing discussion of implementing programs to encourage physician adoption and use of EMRs as well as to enhance the quality of care delivered. An example of such a program that provides financial incentives to providers for significant improvements in care quality through the use of HIT is the *Bridges to Excellence* program. "[The] Bridges to Excellence® (BTE) is a not-for-profit organization that designs and creates programs that encourage physicians and physician practices to deliver safer, more effective and efficient care by giving them financial and other incentives to do so."[10] To achieve further incremental care quality improvements, individuals should also be alerted to their health maintenance and chronic disease management requirements through an ePHR and similarly incented for adherence to their care regimens. This would not only improve overall care quality, but would also enhance the physician adoption of EMRs and individuals' adoption of ePHRs.

Health insurers also require patient information to pay claims. The cost and time involved in claims processing substantially increases for the processing of requests for patient records. If all the information were immediately available through an ePHR, a health insurer could immediately (and easily) access the needed data to adjudicate a claim, reducing processing time and expense substantially.

Employers would benefit substantially from the availability of ePHR systems. The estimated cost savings from the availability of complete patient information is about 8 percent of healthcare costs.[11] These savings predominantly accrue to employers. In addition, the more effective application of prevention and screening that would be possible with ePHR systems, along with better management of chronic diseases, would result in a healthier workforce and reduced productivity loss from illness. In addition to the one time cost savings from ePHR systems, there is also evidence that wellness programs coupled with PHR information can reduce the growth of healthcare costs over time.[12] Since rising healthcare costs are a serious competitive issue for all U.S. companies, it is not an exaggeration to say that ePHR systems are important to help to ensure the future ability of the U.S. to compete successfully in the global economy. For example, supporting employees in their behavioral change efforts (for which employers have begun to use financial incentives and disincentives) to lose weight, stop smoking, etc., could be very helpful in preventing disease and reducing costs.

Other stakeholders would also benefit from ePHR availability. Post-marketing surveillance by pharmaceutical firms and medical device manufacturers would be less expensive and more comprehensive in its coverage, allowing problems to be detected sooner. Medical research of all types would benefit from enhanced ability to find and recruit eligible patients for clinical trials. Public health would enjoy the ability to closely monitor patterns of disease, allowing earlier detection of outbreaks. This latter application has been proven in community environments with access to laboratory results only.[13] Given the possibility of bioterrorism, the ability to continuously monitor health care information has become much more important and is now an issue of national security.

Of all the healthcare stakeholders, consumers are likely to enjoy the greatest benefits from ePHR systems. The benefits of improved quality of care and reduced likelihood of medical errors are obvious and significant to every person. However, the reduced costs secondary to improved efficiency will also benefit consumers in terms of both lower premiums for healthcare insurance coverage as well as avoiding co-payments for services that are duplicative or unnecessary once more complete information is available. Furthermore, consumers will benefit from the ability to better manage their health through the availability of reminders and other value-added applications enabled by ePHR systems. In addition, being able to effectively assert control over the use and disclosure of health information will provide significant peace of mind and allay many current concerns about lack of health privacy. Having large repositories of ePHR information will facilitate research into improved diagnosis and treatment and facilitate healthcare transformation toward personalized medicine. Finally, consumers will also value the ability to share health information with loved ones who are helping to manage their care.

CONCLUSIONS

In terms of ePHR business sustainability, there are four key issues that must be addressed: (1) completeness and reliability of information; (2) trust; (3) critical mass; and (4) compelling business case.

Sustainability is a function of value—and the information in ePHRs must be substantially complete in order to create that value. In fact, it could be argued that an ePHR that is only 50 percent complete is worse than none at all since the available information may be misleading. It is a general characteristic of medical information that it must be relatively complete before being truly useful. For example, an immunization record is of little value to a provider unless it is dependably complete. The absence of a required immunization in an incomplete record can just as easily be due to missing information as missing administration of a vaccine. Therefore, it is not helpful in aiding clinical decisions.

The information in an ePHR must also be reliable. Manual transcription of information by the patient is error-prone and will not be trusted by providers. To provide completeness and reliability, an ePHR must receive ongoing electronic updates from all existing sources of medical information.

Trust is an essential element to sustainability. In its absence, an ePHR system will not be used and therefore will not have value. The information contained in the ePHR must be trusted by all users. In addition, the consumer must have control over any and all access to the contents of the ePHR. However, to ensure trust by providers, the consumer must not be able to alter information loaded directly from other sources. By providing consumer control, the organization holding the ePHR need only be trusted as the "agent" of the consumer to carry out his/her instructions with respect to access. Although this is by no means a trivial level of trust, it is reasonably attainable (as has been done through regulation in the financial industry). If an ePHR system is envisioned wherein the repository organization makes decisions about data release without consumer consent, the trust problem is vastly increased (and may become untenable) as such a high level of trust is extremely difficult to both establish and sustain.

To assure trust, the organization holding the ePHR must also be independent of other entities, including healthcare stakeholders and employers. An organization that is not independent is subject to real or potential coercion with respect to access to information by the overseeing entity. This does not mean that healthcare stakeholders and employers cannot provide sponsorship for the costs of an ePHR. However, if such sponsorship takes the form of directly creating the ePHR organization, trust will be a serious problem. A better solution is to allow the sponsored consumer to choose an ePHR organization and direct the sponsor's funds to that organization to cover all or part of the costs.

There must be a critical mass of ePHR users to assure sustainability. This is not only for financial reasons (i.e., that a large number of customers are needed to offset the substantial fixed costs of a sophisticated ePHR system). It also relates to the issue of process disruption for the providers. If only a small fraction of a physician's patients are using an ePHR, then accessing such data becomes a time-consuming "exception" that interferes with regular workflow. Ideally, ePHR data would automatically populate the clinician's EMR for every patient, with the source(s) of all information clearly indicated. When asked, providers typically express a strong preference that an ePHR be "ubiquitous" as quickly as possible so that they can accommodate their procedures to its use once and then depend on its availability. Rapidly attaining such a critical mass in a community is a very significant challenge.

Finally, while there are a number of approaches to the business case for ePHRs, a "compelling" business case has yet to emerge, particularly for consumers. In order to ensure rapid ePHR adoption by a substantial majority of the consumers in a community, the benefits must be persuasive enough to drive the required behavior change. Recent examples of rapid consumer adoption of technology driven by compelling benefits include cell phones and the iPod™ music player. The current ePHR business models based on subscription fees, sponsorship and advertising have not yet proven sufficient to engage large numbers of consumers, given the currently available ePHR features and functions. Until adoption is more widespread, it is unlikely that ePHRs will be able to deliver on their substantial potential for improving the quality and efficiency of healthcare.

REFERENCES

1. HealthVault homepage. Microsoft HealthVault Web site. Available at: http://www.healthvault.com. Accessed June 11, 2008.
2. Hersh W. Health care information technology: progress and barriers. *JAMA.* 2004; 292: 2273-2274.
3. Pizzi R. Insurance industry reps reveal PHR plan. HealthcareITNews. December 13, 2006. Available at: http://www.healthcareitnews.com/story.cms?id=6052. Accessed June 12, 2008.
4. Hughes B. Health-care professionals, pharmacies, hospitals gain the public's top trust. The Wall Street Journal, Harris Interactive Health Care Research. Volume 3, Issue 2, January 28, 2004.
5. IBM. IBM propels nationwide health information network [press release]. January 23, 2007. Available at: http://www-03.ibm.com/press/us/en/pressrelease/20955.wss. Accessed June 12, 2008.

6. Dossia home page. Available at: http://www.dossia.org/home. Accessed June 12, 2008.

7. Accenture. Majority of consumers believe electronic medical records can improve Medical Care, Accenture Survey Finds. Press release. July 20, 2005. Available at: accenture.tekgroup.com/article_display.cfm?article_id=4236. Accessed July 17, 2008.

8. Accenture. Consumers see electronic health records as important factor when choosing a physician and are willing to pay for service. *Accenture Research Finds.* February 27, 2007. Available at: http://newsroom.accenture.com/article_display. cfm?article_id=4509 . Accessed June 12, 2008.

9. Kaiser Permanente. Kaiser Permanente puts personal health care record front and center. Press release. November 6, 2007. Available at: http://ckp.kp.org/newsroom/national/archive/nat_071106_myhealthmanager.html. Accessed June 12, 2008.

10. Bridges to Excellence. "About Us" page. Available at www.bridgestoexcellence.org/Content/ContentDisplay.aspx?ContentID=2. Accessed October 12, 2008.

11. U.S. Department of Health and Human Services. HHS Fact Sheet – HIT Report at-a-glance. July 21, 2004. Available at: http://www.hhs.gov/news/press/2004pres/20040721.html. Accessed June 12, 2008.

12. U.S. Department of Health and Human Services. Greater Ohama Packing Company Simply Well Program. Available at: http://www.ncvhs.hhs.gov/050106p5.pdf. Accessed June 12, 2008.

13. Overhage JM, Suico J, McDonald CJ. Electronic laboratory reporting: barriers, solutions and findings. *J Public Health Manag Pract.* 2001; 7(6):60-66.

Chapter 10

Conclusions

NEED FOR ePHRS

Over the past several decades, there has been a geometric expansion of medical knowledge. We know more, see more and can do more than ever before. Previously unknown interventions such as hybrid PET/CAT scans, coronary artery angioplasty, laparoscopic tumor ablation, stents and bypass grafts, joint replacement, fiber-optic colonoscopy, lithotripsy, micro-implanted medical devices and mass immunization have become routine. The result has been an expansion of the effective capabilities of healthcare diagnosis, prevention and treatment.

To maintain competence and expertise in the face of exponentially growing medical knowledge, healthcare professionals have become increasingly specialized and sub-specialized to the point where even healthy adults are typically under the care of multiple providers (e.g., internist, ophthalmologist, dermatologist, gastroenterologist, cardiologist, gynecologist and urologist). The days of receiving most of your care directly from a single general practitioner or family physician are long gone. The current practice of medicine "... depends upon the decision-making capacity and reliability of autonomous individual practitioners, for classes of problems that routinely exceed the bounds of unaided human cognition."[1]

Despite the expansion of our medical knowledge base and treatment capabilities, we are just beginning to understand the intricate relationship of genetics and behavior and how they affect health and wellness. As our understanding of this intricate association matures we will be able to apply current and expanding treatment and prevention capabilities in a fashion that is specific to each individual. A transformation in our understanding and practice of medicine toward personalized medicine will occur, when the manner of documentation and communication throughout all medical constituents is transformed as well.

Yet, as this unprecedented transformation in medical care has occurred, little has changed in our patterns of documentation and communication. Healthcare continues to use paper, and for those that use electronic media, health information exchange is limited though growing. Information about care received elsewhere is often requested, sometimes received, but rarely fully integrated into the records. The result is that no one—neither the patient nor any provider—has access to a consumer's complete health record. Furthermore, even if all the paper records were available, the information could not be sorted, arranged and processed into readily usable forms. The vision of complete electronic records for all patients at all points of care continues to be elusive.

It is no wonder, then, that the healthcare sector performs so poorly, with inconsistent delivery of recommended care and high rates of medical errors that often compromise patient safety. Immediate availability of comprehensive health records when and where needed is essential if we hope to improve healthcare quality. In addition, it has been estimated that the annual national savings could exceed $130 billion, about 8% of current healthcare spending.[2]

Access to information helps consumers understand the implications of new medical knowledge to them personally. The availability of comprehensive individual health records opens the door to automated delivery of a wide variety of customized consumer health reminders that can encourage individuals to comply with their medical regimens and practice healthy behaviors. Additionally, the availability and use of medical information on the Internet, public awareness regarding healthcare quality and choices, and knowledge of the costs of healthcare as consumers increasingly become responsible for paying part of these costs, create a market for a comprehensive tool which incorporates PHI with access to such information. Consumers want secure comprehensive electronic records to which they can have access and from which they can control the flow of their health information.

Such a PHR is illustrated in Figure 10-1, where information flows into the PHR from a comprehensive array of the healthcare constituents and information sources with which this individual interacts. In addition, she can enter any personal behavioral information, and network through her PHR with other individuals that share her health conditions, or interests in wellness. She may choose to allow her de-identified data to be used for national (or international) research. She directs and controls the flow of her data, or selected parts of her data, to these and any other healthcare constituents. These constituents and information sources might include multiple providers, her selected pharmacies, her insurer, her home scale and blood pressure monitor.

Figure 10-1. Consumer-Directed Personal Health Records

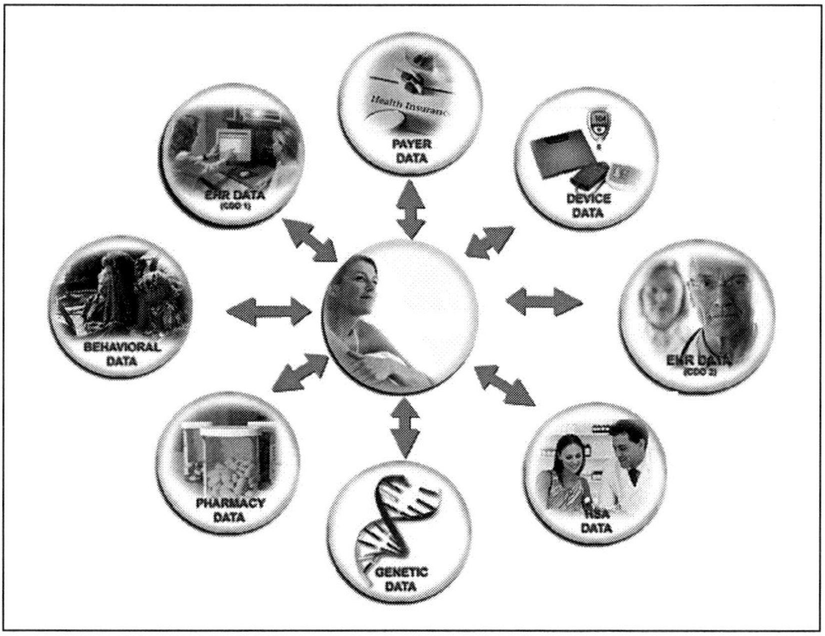

U.S. healthcare is at a critical juncture. Brilliant medical innovations coming out of this country have not translated into overall improvements in national healthcare quality. The adoption of HIT and the ability to capture and appropriately and securely disseminate data electronically will facilitate improved healthcare quality and reduce costs. HIT will also further medical innovation through enhanced data capture and analysis.

PHR, A DISRUPTIVE TECHNOLOGY?

The PHR represents a new model within HIT: the ability for the healthcare consumer to control the collection, storage, and dissemination of their information.

The PHR market is rapidly evolving with access now available through health plans, providers, and commercial PHRs such as HealthVault, Dossia, Google, and many others. The consumer increasingly will be able to choose to store their information on platforms that facilitate data transfer to interfaced healthcare constituents. While consumers continue to be concerned about their data privacy and security, certification of such systems is on the horizon. The key objective of PHR certification, as determined by the CCHIT PHR Advisory Task Force, will be patient privacy and security.

The goals of an ideal ePHR include:
- Encouraging individuals to focus on health and wellness, preventive medicine and supporting their adoption of healthy behaviors.
- Improving the chronic care management of individuals and supporting these individuals to comply with their treatment plans.
- Creating the ability for a provider to access critical clinical information in the event of an individual's need for emergency treatment.
- Enabling the accumulation of clinical, behavioral, genetic and outcome data to support analysis to create predictive modeling and personalized medicine and allowing individuals to decide if they want their de-identified data to be included in this work.

- Empowering individuals to make informed healthcare decisions where they can select centers of excellence with the best outcomes and lowest costs by utilizing transparent provider information regarding outcomes and costs.
- Supporting individuals to become informed regarding their conditions and results.
- Supporting individuals to make behavioral changes through ePHR tools and education regarding their own behavioral influences on their long-term health outcomes and health-wealth consequences.
- Creating a consumer–provider partnership toward achieving enhanced preventive medicine practices, healthy behaviors and medical regimen compliance through improved communication and education.

Healthcare in the U.S. is in the midst of unstructured transformation driven not by a master plan but rather by the multiplicity of interests in, and groups affected by, the healthcare economy. This is an appropriate reflection of a market economy that allows the slow development of products that meet the needs and desires of consumers. PHRs will both transform and be transformed by this process. At the present time, HIT in general and PHRs specifically are enabling technologies for healthcare transformation. If the ideal PHR is achieved and can fulfill the goals cited above, the PHR will be a disruptive technology in healthcare. It will change an individual's responsibilities and empowerment regarding their health, their relationships with their providers and other healthcare constituents. Finally, PHRs will alter healthcare through enabling data acquisition and centralization of an enhanced data set, thereby further facilitating medical transformation toward personalized medicine.

REFERENCES

1. Masys DR. Knowledge management: keeping up with the growing knowledge. Presented at the 2001 IOM Annual Meeting. Washington, DC. Available at: http://www.iom.edu/subpage.asp?id=7774. Accessed June 12, 2008.
2. Pan E, Johnston D, Walker J, Adler-Milstein J, Bates D, Middleton B. *The Value of Healthcare Information Exchange and Interoperability.* Boston: Center for Information Technology Leadership; 2004.

Acronyms Used in This Book

AAFP	American Academy of Family Physicians
AAP	American Academy of Pediatrics
ACP	American College of Physicians
ADT	admission discharge transfer
AHIC	American Health Information Community
AHIMA	American Health Information Management Association
AMDIS	Association of Medical Directors of Information Systems
AMIA	American Medical Informatics Association
ANSI	American National Standards Institute
AOA	American Osteopathic Association
CCHIT	Certification Commission for Healthcare Information Technology
CMS	Centers for Medicare & Medicaid Services
CPT	current procedural terminology
DMZ	demilitarized zone
EHR	electronic health record
EHRA	Electronic Health Record Association
EHRVA	Electronic Health Record Vendors Association (now referred to as the Electronic Health Record Association)
EMR	electronic medical record
ePHR	electronic personal health record
ERISA	Employment Retirement Income Security Act
FAQs	frequently asked questions
GDP	gross domestic product
HHS	U.S. Department of Health and Human Services
HIE	health information exchange
HIMSS	Healthcare Information and Management Systems Society

HIPAA	Health Insurance Portability and Accountability Act of 1996
HIT	healthcare information technology
HL7	Health Level 7
HMO	health maintenance organization
HRA	health risk assessment
ICE	in case of emergency
ICT	Health Information and Communications Technology
IDN	independent delivery network
IOM	Institute of Medicine
IS	information services
ISO	International Organization for Standardization
MHV	My HealtheVet (Veterans Administration's ePHR)
NAHIT	National Alliance for Health Information Technology
NCVHS	National Committee on Vital and Health Statistics
NHII	National Health Information Infrastructure
OECD	Organization for Economic Co-operation and Development
ONC	Office of the National Coordinator for Health Information Technology
OTS	off the shelf
P4P	pay for performance
PBHR	payor-based health records
PBM	pharmacy benefits manager
PHI	personal health information
PHR	personal health record
RHIO	regional health information organization
RWJ	Robert Wood Johnson Foundation
SDO	standards development organization
SNOMED	Systemated Nomenclature of Human and Veterinary Medicine
VA	U.S. Department of Veterans Affairs

Index